COLLECTING AND STUDYING
Mushrooms, Toadstools and Fungi

COLLECTING AND STUDYING
Mushrooms, Toadstools and Fungi

by Alan Major

Illustrated by Barbara Prescott

ARCO PUBLISHING COMPANY, INC.
New York

589.2
M

Published 1975 by Arco Publishing Company, Inc.
219 Park Avenue South, New York, N.Y. 10003
Copyright © 1974 by Alan Major
All rights reserved
Library of Congress Catalog Card Number 74-19896
ISBN 0-668-03725-3

Printed in Great Britain

Contents

Dedication

This book is humbly dedicated to the memory of the late George (Will) Coxhead, botanist and mycologist, who nurtured the interest of the author when just beginning the study of these subjects and to whom the author owes almost everything regarding his natural history career.

And to Joan Coxhead, a friend of many years, as a token of thanks and small recompense for her kindness and generosity.

Acknowledgments

The author acknowledges his gratitude and sincere thanks to Mr D. A. L. Davies, author of the paper 'The Preservation of Larger Fungi by Freeze Drying' for his assistance and for permission to freely quote from this source, and to Professor A. G. Morton, senior editor of *Transactions of the British Mycological Society* in which Mr Davies's paper was originally published in 1962 (Vol. 45) for kindly allowing me to quote. The author also offers his thanks to Mr D. M. Dring, The Herbarium, Royal Botanic Gardens, Kew, Surrey, for assistance with information, and to Mrs Christine Hartley, Nanaimo, British Columbia, Canada, for information regarding North American species. Photographs 1–14 are by R. G. Argent and 15 and 16 by N.H.P.A. Lastly, but by no means least, the author acknowledges the co-operation received from Miss Barbara Prescott in her skilful illustration of the fungus examples.

List of Colour Plates

Plate 10 An **Earth Star** (*Geastrum fornicatum*). Note how the exoperidium has split into lobes, like legs, to lift the fungus above the habitat.

Plate 11 Some fine examples of the **Shaggy Parasol, Ragged Parasol** or **Shaggy Lepiota** (*Lepiota rhacodes*). They often occur in gardens where there is humus rich soil and compost heaps.

Plate 12 A dense cluster of **Sulphur Tuft** or **Sulphur Top** (*Hypholoma fasciculare*) on the trunk of a dead elm tree.

Plate 13 A group of *Pholiota spectabilis*, a striking golden brown species that occurs in tufts on broadleafed and conifer trees and stumps.

Plate 14 The **Common Stinkhorn** or **Wood Witch** (*Phallus impudicus*), which occurs in woodlands and wooded gardens and makes its presence known by its unpleasant aroma, attractive to flies, but repellant to human beings!

Plate 15 The **Fly Agaric** or **Fly Amanita** (*Amanita muscaria*) immediately recognized as the species used in children's fairy tale picture books, but also a poisonous relative of the Death Cap. It was named because it was formerly used in milk as a fly killer.

Plate 16 The edible **Field** or **Meadow Mushroom** (*Agaricus campestris*), traditionally the most popular fungi to consume in Britain. Note its differences with that of the Death Cap in Plate 7.

Introduction

Fungi have an aura evoking mystery and curiosity, allied with a touch of fear for the poisonous – or suspected poisonous – species among them. It is perhaps principally for this latter reason that they are not as popular for study as are other forms of wild life; I therefore set out to attempt to prove that these flowerless plants can be extremely fascinating.

Neither will the keen amateur mycologist – the collector of fungi – stop when his fascination has been satisfied, for it is then that he will realize the truth that here is still a field in which the lone amateur can explore and research, for much detailed work is yet to be done on fungi. For example, in some of the following descriptions the colour of the spores is not given – simply because it is not known.

Certain confusions also arise in the nomenclature of fungi, many species having completely different names in North America from those by which they are known in Britain – while there are rare cases of the same name applying to two distinct fungi. To ease this confusion I have indicated which country uses which name – where no country is stated the name is understood in both.

Finally, may I appeal to the common–sense of collectors not to denude an area of a particular species: conservation also applies to the world of the fungus.

ALAN MAJOR

1 Fungi and Their Development

There are some two hundred thousand species of fungus in the world. Within this vast assortment, ranging from the Giant Puffball, the size of a football, to the microscopic organisms that cause blight on potatoes or give us penicillin, there is a wealth of variety and of interest, and it is one of the few fields of operation where the amateur can still hope to make new discoveries.

By definition, the Latin word *fungus* means 'a mushroom', 'a spongy excrescence', and was used for the larger species. This term was also derived from the Greek word 'sphonggos' or 'sphoggos', sponge, referring to the sponge-like structure of some of the species. The word 'mushroom' is derived from the French 'mousseron', its etymology being doubtful and perhaps deriving from 'mousse', moss. Other versions are 'muscheron', 'mouscheron' and from these it is easy to understand how the country name of 'musheroon' originated.

The etymology of the word 'toadstool' is unknown and does not have a scientific meaning. From an early version of 'tad(e)stole' – the Old English name for the toad being 'tadde' – the fungi were known later as 'todestoles'. The word may have simply originated from the rural belief that toads were venomous, that fungi developed from poisonous substances in the earth and that both occurred together in shady, damp and 'unwholesome' places.

There has also been considerable confusion over what is classed as a mushroom and what a toadstool. The belief is very widespread that mushrooms are the edible species of fungi (dangerously inaccurate as I explain later in this chapter) and toadstools are the poisonous fungi. Alternatively 'mushroom' is applied only to the Common Edible Field or Meadow Mushroom (*Agaricus campestris*) and to several related edible and poisonous species, the definition of 'toadstool' being any

15

fungi other than mushrooms, especially those of supposedly poisonous species. I have followed this latter system and used the word mushroom only where correctly applicable and have not used the word toadstool at all, using instead the names by which international mycologists will know the fungi.

In the vegetable kingdom fungi are classed as simple plants, and differ from all others in several aspects. One of these is that they lack the green colouring matter – chlorophyll – and cannot manufacture their own food supply. To counter this, fungi have to obtain their organic material from other sources, by existing upon living plants and animals as parasites, or by living upon dead or decaying plant or animal remains as saprophytes. This does not mean that a fungus always destroys its host. Mycorhiza fungi or 'fungus roots' form with plants such as wild orchids and forest trees, a partnership which is so finely developed that it is of mutual benefit to both, mycorhiza in the soil being essential for orchid seed germination.

Fungi in their different forms have various uses, some of which are beneficial, while others are destructive. That some species are edible is well-known; equally that some are poisonous causing death or sickness. Some provide drugs for use in fighting human disease – penicillin is an example – while others cause infections, such as ringworm and athletes' foot.

Fungi are valuable scavengers, breaking down and removing dead organic matter, but they can also attack the tissues of living trees and plants. Others occur as moulds on stored foods like jam, bread, cheese and butter, as blight on potatoes, as rusts on wheat and garden flowers, as mildew on plants, fabrics and paper, as smuts on cereals, or as the 'dry rot' in buildings. Nor may it be forgotten that yeasts, unicellular micro-fungi, are used in brewing and bread-making.

Equally, there has been much dangerous confusion on how to establish if gathered specimens are poisonous or edible. There is no test which will provide this information, the safe way – indeed the only way – being to identify the fungus species correctly. If there is the slightest doubt, a specimen should not be considered as edible: one should never take a chance on eating the unknown. Though it probably will not kill, the result could be several unpleasant hours or days.

16

Let us consider some of the so-called 'tests', beginning with one from the illustrious Mrs Beeton who, in her cookery book, should have shown more sense. She claimed that 'a silver sixpence should be placed in the pan when cooking mushrooms for safety's sake', in the belief that poisonous species turned the coin black whereas safe species did not. Similarly, poisonous fungi were supposed to turn silverware black. This is not correct. The poisonous Death Cap, for example, does *not* tarnish silver utensils.

Another error is that the caps of edible fungi peel, whereas poisonous species do not. Yet the species that causes 90 per cent of deaths from poisoning, the Death Cap (*Amanita phalloides*) peels easily.

A further mistaken belief is that the brightly coloured species are poisonous, while the plain white or creamy species are safe. Yet species such as Chanterelle (*Cantharellus cibarius*) and Wood Blewits (*Tricholoma nudum*), although attractively bright egg-yellow and lilac respectively, are safe, while the common yellowish-olive and white Death Cap (*Amanita phalloides*), and the rare Fool's Mushroom (*Amanita verna*) and Destroying Angel (*Amanita virosa*) – the last two being completely white are all deadly.

Equally incorrect is the belief that all poisonous species become a different colour if bruised or cut, although it is true of some fungi, the Yellow-staining Mushroom (*Agaricus xanthoderma*) quickly changing from white to yellow where it is bruised, *Boletus satanas* turning bluish-green, and *Boletus luridus* rapidly becoming vivid blue when damaged. The latex or 'milk' exuded by the species of Milk Caps also changes colour on exposure to air, an example being the orange latex of the edible Saffron Milk Cap (*Lactarius deliciosus*) which turns green. None of these colour changes has any significance in defining poisonous from edible species and is a purely chemical action.

Probably more widespread in the past than now was the belief that fungi which are partially eaten by wild animals, slugs and snails, can also be safely eaten by human beings. This too is incorrect, since animals such as deer, badgers, squirrels and rabbits with their less sensitive digestive systems can eat without ill-effect fungi that are poisonous to man: their stomachs are able to neutralize the toxic properties. The mere sight of slugs feeding on a fungus should make most people avoid the specimen.

There is also no proven method of neutralizing poisonous constituents and rendering them edible. For this reason the old practice of soaking specimens in water with salt and vinegar, and then boiling, is risky, and if it is used on edible species as a precaution it affects their flavour. It should be unnecessary to add that the mycologist, after handling fungi with bare hands, should always wash thoroughly before eating. He should not forget that of the Death Cap, even the spores are poisonous and only a tiny amount is needed to cause illness.

Of the six thousand species of fungus recorded in the British Isles, about a dozen are poisonous enough to cause vomiting, stomach pain, colic, diarrhoea, vertigo, sweating, pupil dilation and a feeling of cold in the limbs, and from the dangerous species some of these effects are able to cause liver degeneration, paralysis of the nervous system, coma and an agonizing death. While several species make delicious dishes, many are unpalatable, perhaps through being woody, leathery and tough, or having a bitter, acrid flavour, others again being too fleshy and tasteless and so worthless as food.

It must also be remembered that even edible fungi can cause indigestion in otherwise healthy people and some persons may be allergic to species which are harmless to others; obviously, people who cannot digest fungi easily should avoid eating them. Sometimes it is only one species which causes illness; or it may be one fungus family. Causes of discomfort and indigestion are many, from simply eating too many, or eating them with indigestible foods, to the fungi themselves being past maturity, or incorrectly cooked, probably through being too damp. Fungi may also cause illness if alcohol is taken at the same meal, an example being the purplish-red skin discoloration which is the temporary result of eating the Ink Cap (*Coprinus atramentarius*) with alcohol.

A person showing any of the symptoms up to twelve hours after eating fungi should immediately seek medical assistance. Vomit with fungi fragments, or any remains of the fungi themselves should be retained for possible identification, and to know the poisonous properties contained and the antidote

18

required. The victim should be given glasses of salt–water emetic and covered to maintain body warmth.

I strongly emphasize again that the only way to know edible from poisonous species is to identify them correctly. The entire specimen, even that portion in the earth or habitat – the volva – should be collected to check all its characteristics for accurate identification. Collectors who intend to eat some of their finds should, until they become more skilled or receive guidance from experts, concentrate only on the easily recognized species. Rather than gather specimens which are old, partly decomposed or too wet, one should use only fresh, young fungi, avoiding however, the wild, undeveloped 'button' fungi unless one is certain of their identity. Dried with a cloth after washing – one should never prepare wet fungi – they should then be cooked as soon as possible, taking care not to over or undercook: it is this latter fault which makes the edible species indigestible. Neither should the species be mixed, either in the kitchen or on the table, nor reheated after a first cooking.

Despite the shortage of food during the Second World War the British still retain a natural reluctance to eat wild fungi, except for a few varieties like the Common Field Mushroom (*Agaricus campestris*), Horse Mushroom (*Agaricus arvensis*), Cep (*Boletus edulis*) Wood Blewit (*Tricholoma nudum*) Blewit or Blue Leg (*Tricholoma personatum*) and Morel (*Morchella esculenta*). Our fungus consumption is concentrated on specially cultivated 'button' mushrooms, bought from greengrocers as a savoury supplement to the main meal at breakfast or dinner, and as tins of mushroom soup or sauce, or ketchup or mushroom powder flavouring. On the Continent and in the Far East it is a different story with numerous wild species consumed in various ways, some of these being specially cultivated on fungus farms and sold in shops and markets.

Fungi contain 80 to 90 per cent water, $1\frac{1}{2}$ to 5 per cent nitrogen, up to 9 per cent carbohydrates, up to $2\frac{1}{2}$ per cent sugars, up to 1 per cent fats and about the same amount of mineral matter, especially potassium salts and phosphates. These totals are only a rough approximation and vary among species. The value of fungi as a food is open to question, but

19

some species do also contain varying quantities of vitamins B_1, B_2, C, D, and nicotinic acid.

Returning to the differences between higher plants and fungi, a major distinction is that plants reproduce by seeds, having an embryo, whereas fungi reproduce by spores, without an embryo. These spores, dust dry, viscous or slimy, round or oval, smooth or wrinkled, are so minute that a single one, which may be less than 10/25,000 of an inch long, can be examined only under a microscope. When heaped, the drier spores may take on the characteristics of a very fine powder which is undetectable to the finger and which has been compared with the finest milled cocoa (Fig 1). Fungi produce enormous numbers of spores, the vast majority of which fail to germinate by falling on to hostile habitats. In the several days of its maturity a Field or Meadow Mushroom may produce between 1,600 million and 1,800 million spores, while the mature Giant Puffball and Bracket Fungus may each yield over 7,000 million. Being so microscopic the spores may be carried on air currents at considerable heights and for many hours. The spores of species like the Stinkhorn are also taken away on visiting insects or animals which feed on it.

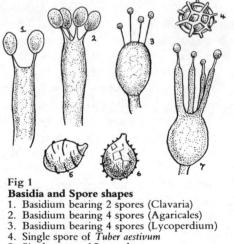

Fig 1
Basidia and Spore shapes
1. Basidium bearing 2 spores (Clavaria)
2. Basidium bearing 4 spores (Agaricales)
3. Basidium bearing 4 spores (Lycoperdium)
4. Single spore of *Tuber aestivum*
5. Single spore of **Lactarius**
6. Single spore of **Russula**
7. Tremellales

20

These distribution methods can be demonstrated by suddenly squeezing a mature Puffball or pressing the shoe against it; while a yellowish-brown cloud of spores is ejected into the air from the top of the fungus, a number will also have adhered to the fingers or shoe. In the case of the self-digesting species, rain may also distribute the spores.

In the Gill Fungus, the spores are produced by the gills on the underside of the cap; if a vertical section is cut through a gill and examined under a compound microscope it will show that its surface consists of a compact layer of minute, club-shaped projecting cells or structures called *basidia*, the tip of each of these having four narrow pointed stalks called *sterigmata*, each of which produces a spore, although in some species, such as the Cultivated Mushroom, there may be only two *sterigmata*. Between the larger *basidia* are some shorter, sterile cells called *paraphyses*, the whole fertile compact layer of tissue being known as the *hymenium* (Fig 2).

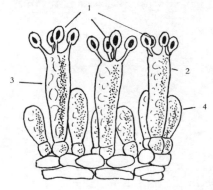

Fig 2
Section of hymenium
1. Spores
2. Sterigmata
3. Basidia
4. Paraphyses

As soon as they are mature the spores are liberated by being expelled violently from the *sterigmata* on the *basidia* by means of a water-drop mechanism and descend through the vertical space between the gills to be transported by air or other means. The spores do not casually drop out as might be thought.

The anatomy of fungi can differ greatly, some species having their *basidia* not on gills but on 'teeth', or lining the insides of tubes. The Common Puffball (Fig 3) already mentioned, consists of a mass of soft tissue enclosed by a membrane called the *peridium*. This skin itself has two layers;

21

the inner, called the *endoperidium* which has at its top the pore or mouth through which the spores are released; and an outer layer called the *exoperidium* which has a covering of erect spine-like warts which usually fall or rub off as the fungus matures. The entire *peridium* in the Puffballs may be filled with spore-bearing tissue, the *gleba*, while in other species the *gleba* may occupy only the upper part of the *peridium*, the lower part, called the sterile base, having a stem-like shape. There are variations of these differences in other species in the *Gasteromycetes* to which the Puffball belongs – such as the Earth Stars, the Stinkhorns and their relatives.

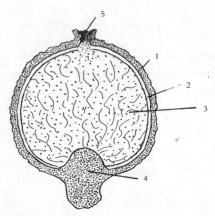

Fig 3
Anatomy of Puffball
1. Exoperidium
2. Endoperidium
3. Gleba
4. Columella
5. Apical pore or mouth

Some fungi *hyphae* – the tiny, thread-like filaments or structures that comprise the *mycelium* and fruit body of the fungi – also grow reproductive organs in or upon which are borne the spores of the succeeding generation. There are two types of spore – asexual and sexual. Asexual spores usually produce descendants which are identical with the parents. One example is the spores of Bread Mould which are produced in a stalked rounded spore case or *sporangium* (Fig 4) and are transported on air currents. Another example is the *zoospores* of Water Mould, produced in a *sporangium* at the tip of a *hypha* and which, having tail-like *flagella*, are able to move away from the parent before germinating. They are also produced sexually, this fungus being a parasite on fish. Other asexual spores are produced by the breaking off, budding off, or segmenting of portions of a *hyphae* tip, each portion

22

becoming a *sporangium*. These may also divide into *zoospores* which eventually develop into *hyphae*, or the *sporangium* itself may germinate into a new *hypha*. This type of spore is produced very rapidly and accounts for the fast development of moulds which appear on bread, potatoes, vetetables, strawberries and other fruit.

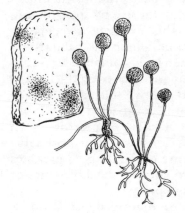

Fig 4
Sporangium of Bread Mould

Sexual spores are reproduced by the extension of special branches or organs, one being classified as male, the other female, containing two similar cells or *gametes* that fuse to form a *zygote*, which is a resting stage and germinates later (Fig 5). Alternatively, cells from the male organ, the *antheridium*, fuse with eggs in the female organ, the *oogonium*.

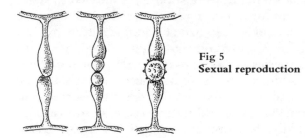

Fig 5
Sexual reproduction

To germinate, the spore must be deposited on a favourable habitat that has enough nutritious food and sufficient

23

moisture, plus an amenable temperature. From the spore a small, thin, tube-like projection, the germ-tube or *hypha*, grows horizontally, mingling with the *hyphae* of surrounding spores to form a thread or a more complex mass known as the *mycelium*, or spawn, which is usually white or brown and can on occasion be brightly coloured or dark.

During their development, the *hyphae* produce chemicals which digest the food around them for use by the growing fungus fruit body. In some species this *mycelium* or vegetative phase can persist for several seasons where the habitats are untouched by severe frost as in deep layers of fallen leaves. In other species the *mycelium* cells may produce extra thick walls to resist hard winter weather. To survive during prolonged drought or cold the *mycelium* become compacted into *sclerotia* – hard rounded masses, from pea-size upwards, with thickened outer walls, that stay dormant until hospitable conditions return. In this way some of the fungoid parasites like rusts and mildews are able to survive the adversities of winter and reappear the following spring.

The time taken for a fungus to mature depends on its species. The Field or Meadow Mushroom may take as little as seven or eight weeks, whereas some of the larger Bracket Fungi may take several years. Although the fruit body may appear in a relatively short time, though not quite 'overnight', it must be remembered that the unseen early stages of immaturity take considerably longer.

As an experiment to discover the gestation period of colonization, a damp bonfire site should be allowed to stand undisturbed, except for removing large weeds. In the course of time this site should be colonized by fungi. Alternatively a plot of land could be dug over and left fallow, while to encourage other species a newly sawn tree branch could be left undisturbed. Within a few months these sites should be carrying fungi, assuming only that the season is correct and there is no extraneous factor inhibiting spore germination.

To understand the development of a gill-bearing fungus in the *Agaricaceae* family, the type with which this book is mainly concerned, it is essential to know the parts of a fungus and their function, and perhaps the best way is to follow the *mycelium* through its growth stages (Fig 6).

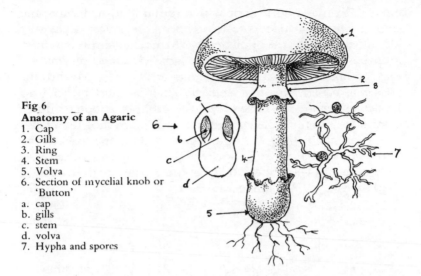

Fig 6
Anatomy of an Agaric
1. Cap
2. Gills
3. Ring
4. Stem
5. Volva
6. Section of mycelial knob or 'Button'
a. cap
b. gills
c. stem
d. volva
7. Hypha and spores

The first appearance of the fungus-to-be is in the small compact pinhead-like knobs which sprout from the *mycelium*, gradually changing to oval or club-shaped as they progress towards the habitat surface, the upper end of the knobs swelling as the stem and cap take shape. This is the 'button' stage of the Common Field or Meadow Mushroom, when the plate-like gills are formed by the *hyphae* growing into the ring-shaped cavity under the cap. *Hyphae* also grow upwards from the stem and on meeting those growing downwards from the cap edge, create a membrane that covers the developing gills as the spores form. The button stage continues as the mushroom develops within the membrane, the cap increasing as the gills elongate further. The membrane now ceases to broaden but the cap goes on increasing until it bursts through the stretched membrane which remains on the stem as the ring. In the Amanita fungi the entire immature fruit body or *sporophore* is enclosed and formed within a fairly thin outer membrane known as the universal veil or general veil.

Inside the upper part the cap is at first dome-shaped, with a series of slits in the underside, the walls between these slits eventually becoming the gills. On the maturing Amanita the cap bursts through the enclosing outer membrane – the universal veil – a portion of which remains at the base of the stem to form a loose sheath or cup, the *volva*, a positive identification to the poisonous Amanita family, whose members include the Death Cap (*Amanita phalloides*), Destroying Angel (*Amanita virosa*) and Fool's Mushroom (*Amanita verna*). In other species, such as the Panther Cap (*Amanita pantherina*) the volva just remains as one or more girdles around the swollen stem base, or, as in the False Death Cap (*Amanita citrina*), a single ridge on the upper part of the bulbous stem base (Fig 7). Some of the torn *Universal veil* may also remain as wart-like patches on the surface of the cap, as in the Fly Agaric (*Amanita muscaria*).

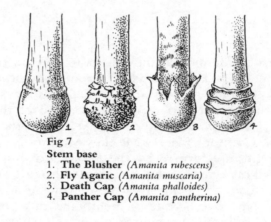

Fig 7
Stem base
1. **The Blusher** (*Amanita rubescens*)
2. **Fly Agaric** (*Amanita muscaria*)
3. **Death Cap** (*Amanita phalloides*)
4. **Panther Cap** (*Amanita pantherina*)

The circular gill-cavity is closed in the early growth stages of the *Amanitas* and the Common Field Mushroom, the *gills* being covered by a thin membrane from the edge of the cap to the stem, the so-called partial veil. As the fruit body or *sporophore* develops, the universal veil is burst open, followed by the rupture of the partial veil round the edge of the cap. This partial veil if it remains, forms a spreading or hanging collar around the upper part of the stem and is known as the ring or annulus.

In certain species, such as those of the Cortinarius, the partial veil has cobweb-like filaments, called the *cortina*, from the edge of the cap to the stem. This veil, however, is usually found complete only in immature examples and by the time the cap is fully extended nothing may remain except a narrow area of *fibrils* or filaments on the stem, or as a slender fringe on the cap edge.

It must be remembered that not all Gill-Fungi have both types of veil. Some may only have a volva, others volva and ring, while others only a ring, details which must be noted at the time of collecting as they are essential to the positive identification of several species.

There are five chief groups of fungi – the *Phycomycetes*, the *Basidiomycetes*, the *Ascomycetes*, the *Fungi Imperfecti*, and the *Myxomycetes* or Slime Moulds.

The Phycomycetes are microscopic algal fungi, related to the algae or seaweeds because they have a similar method of reproduction. Some species are aquatic, producing mobile sperms; others are filamentous, differing from other fungi in that their *hyphae* have no cross-walls, except in the spore branches, which have clearly defined sexual organs. The *mycelium* consists of branched hollow tubes. Some of the Phycomycetes are the major causes of plant diseases – blight on potatoes and tomatoes, rusts on the cabbage family, and mildew on vines.

The Basidiomycetes comprise two very large groups – one containing rusts, smuts and gelatinous jelly and ear fungi, the other, the true *Basidiums*, containing the majority of the large fungi with typical woody, fleshy, or papery fruit bodies. The spores of the Basidiomycetes are developed externally at the tip of short stalks, the *sterigmata*, on the swollen cells or club-shaped structures called *basidia*. These are in a fertile layer called the *hymenium* and are described elsewhere in this chapter.

The true *Basidiums* are also divided into two groups according to the method of producing spores. In one group, the *Hymenomycetes*, the spores are formed on gills, tubes, or spines open to the atmosphere so that they can easily be released from the basidia when mature for distribution by air currents, an example being the Field or Meadow Mushroom. There are also other variations which are explained in the relevant descriptive chapters.

In the second group, the *Gasteromycetes*, the spores develop inside the outer shell of a closed fruit body and are released either through a pore or mouth, or by the disintegration of the entire fruit body, as in the Puffball.

The rusts and smuts within the Basidiomycetes have very complex life cycles and some of the species need two hosts in what may be up to five spore stages. For example, Wheat Rust also attacks barberry as part of its life cycle. Cedar Apple Rust in North America infects apples and junipers as well as cedar, and Pine Blister Rust attacks gooseberry bushes. From this it will be realized that the parasitic rusts and smuts which also attack sweet corn, beans, asparagus, currants and roses, can be serious damaging pests.

The Ascomycetes or Sac Fungi also comprise a very large group, some of which are microscopic. The spores are produced in minute, closed tubes or sacs, called *asci* (Fig 8) forming a closely packed layer, the *hymenium*, in which each *ascus* usually has eight spores, though may have four or less. The asci are borne on various types of fruit bodies as referred to in the relevant descriptions, in some species being produced inside a closed, flask-like structure or receptacle, the *perithecium* the spores when mature being expelled through a pore in the top.

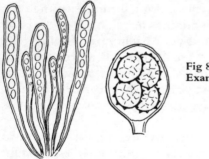

Fig 8
Examples of asci

The *perithecia* may be grouped in a large mass of tissue called a *stroma*, and forming the surface of the fruit body, in which case the openings of the perithecia would be tiny pores on the fruit body's surface. One such group is the Pyrenomycetes. In a second group, the Discomycetes, the exposed hymenium, with the spore-bearing asci, either covers the surface of a fruit body shaped like a club, or lines the interior of a cup-shaped depression, examples being the Morels and Cup Fungi. A third group have the asci within an enclosed, fleshy, tuber-like fruit body, which is under the ground. In this group are the edible Truffles.

Some of the microscopic Sac Fungi are parasites, occurring as powdery mildews on some plants and green mould on citrus fruit, or as mildew on damp walls and leather. Others in the family are valuable: one is yeast; another is used to ripen certain cheeses, while a third is the source of penicillin.

The Fungi Imperfecti, so-called because they produce spores without fusion of sexual cells also form a very large group of microscopic fungi, the life-cycle of many of which is unknown or incomplete, especially in the sexual stages, although it is known that some reproduce by asexual spores carried on the air. Here lies one of those open fields for the amateur mycologist to investigate.

Among the Fungi Imperfecti are the specimens responsible for mildews, the mould which attacks clothing, and the various plant diseases such as blight, leaf spot, fruit rot and wilt. Others among this family infect grasses and give rise to the airborne spores responsible for respiral ailments, athlete's foot, ringworm, and 'Farmer's Lung'.

The Myxomycetes, the Slime Fungi or Slime Moulds are not considered true fungi because of their structure and the differing stages of their life-cycle. For this reason they were formerly classed as Amoebas or *Mycetozoa* (Fungus Animals) instead of plants, but as part of their life-cycle includes a plant-like stage when spores are produced, these curious organisms can be grouped with the fungi: some of them will almost certainly be found by collectors although the majority are microscopic. The Myxomycetes have a vegetative, jelly-like and naked body made of protoplasm – *plasmodium* – which contains numerous nuclei but has no cell walls. They are found in dark wet places, on rotting logs, among decaying leaves, or sometimes in grass that stays fairly wet. One example begins life as an airborne spore which on germination, congregates into a minute swarm-cell, each member equipped with a flagellum for mobility.

This species, which has the added attraction of multiplying by body division, eventually loses its tail-like flagellum, becomes amoeboid, then coalesces into the protoplasmic form. The mature plasmodium eventually changes into the fruiting structures, the *sporangia*, each of which contains the numerous spores. These fruit bodies vary considerably among the species from small, squat masses to open-woven baskets and long stalked structures, the delicately arranged tracery of which is only revealed under a powerful lens. They also vary considerably in colour, from white, yellow, brown and orange, to purple and black. If the plasmodium dries out, perhaps because of dry weather or unexpected drying of its habitat by another cause, it will recover and start to grow again when wetted. For this reason it can be stored easily for examination and the fruit bodies can also be preserved dry for later study.

Fig 9 **Flowers of Tan** (*Fuligo septica*)

The largest Slime Mould is Flowers of Tan (*Fuligo septica*) (Fig 9) found on decayed wood and earth. Measuring up to eight inches in diameter and two inches high, the cushion-shaped fruit body is stalkless and lime-encrusted. In the early stage it is pale tan-coloured, but changes to dark purple as the spore-mass matures and the covering of frail grey lime crust disintegrates and breaks off.

Similar is the two-inch diameter cushion-shaped fruit body of *Reticularia lycoperdon* (British Isles), found on tree stumps and decayed timber. Its dark rusty-red spore mass has a thin covering of silvery grey crust. The Deep-Brown Stemonitis (*Stemonitis splendens*) (North America), found on decaying

30

wood, has a flattish sporangium bearing numerous erect, stiff, hair-like stalks. Dark brown, it measures up to one inch in height. Ceratiomyxa (*Ceratiomyxa fruticulosa*) (Fig 10) (North America), also occurring on rotten wood, does not produce spore cases; instead the spores are borne on erect, branched, club-shaped pillars that form powdery areas on the habitat. Whitish, it grows up to a quarter inch high.

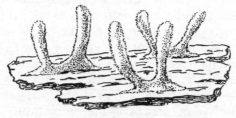

Fig 10 **Ceratiomyxa**

Of these five chief groups of fungus, the Phycomycetes, the Basidiomycetes rusts and smuts, the Fungi Imperfecti and the majority of the Slime Moulds – apart from those described – are microscopic and therefore only likely to be of concern to the research student of mycology. As this book is mainly intended for the amateur collector-cum-naturalist these minute, complex fungi have been omitted in favour of the larger and more easily identified specimens, the Basidiomycetes and Ascomycetes, whose species are fully described in later chapters.

2 How To Collect Fungi

To gather fungus specimens the collector requires only a few basic items, the most important being a suitable container. The ideal choice is a basket, preferably large, wide and open, with a flat bottom and a strong handle. A wicker shopping basket is suitable, an alternative being a gardener's trug. The vasculum used by botanists for plant specimens is not suitable for the more fragile, fleshy specimens of fungus, although it could be used in an emergency for the tough, woody species. To prevent the basketwork bruising the examples, the bottom and sides should be lined with several sheets of clean, plain paper. Though newspaper is an acceptable substitute, a layer of thin foam rubber is a better alternative.

As they are gathered the fungi should be arranged carefully in the basket and rolls of newspaper sheets placed between them. As an added precaution each specimen can be placed carefully in a paper or plastic bag with a few small holes made in it.

If a large number of specimens is discovered in the later stages of an expedition and the basket is already comfortably full, then fresh layers of protective paper should be laid over the earlier samples, which will also avoid the intermingling of different spores. Ideally, of course, one should carry two baskets if there is the possibility of a considerable variety of examples being found; it is better to return home with one empty basket than with one overloaded with specimens that are almost certainly damaged and probably crushed.

The larger, woody or semi-dry species are less fragile and so can be carefully wrapped in clean paper, then if kept separate from the frail specimens in another basket they can be packed more closely.

Small, frail examples can be pinned to lengths of balsa wood or cork firmly fixed into the bottom of a square biscuit tin. Where the specimen is on a twig or leaf, one should push a pin through this as well as through the specimen if there is a likelihood the fungus will break off while being carried.

Very small examples can be placed in glass specimen tubes with a wad of cotton wool at top and bottom.

To remove specimens from their habitat, an old kitchen knife, gardening trowel or builder's pointing trowel are ideal tools, but they are in no way a substitute for the skill which must also be used: one hand should steady the cap and stem throughout the operation. Bracket fungi growing on timber are removable with a sharp penknife, but again considerable care is needed.

In addition to rubber gloves – for some fungi leave an unpleasant aroma – the collector should also equip himself with a pocketbook and pencil (and a few spares!) for those vital on-the-spot notes, particularly if several locations are to be visited. What could be worse than returning home and finding the specimens, though perfectly safe, lacking those necessary identifying details?

Labelling is easy with a few prepared strips of paper to slip in the bag with each specimen, carrying a simple code number or letter which refers to the notebook where all the relevant details should be noted at the time of collecting.

These permanent labelling details should be as comprehensive as possible, including the type of locality – woodland, garden, pasture, sand dune; the actual site in the locality – on dung or compost heap, in grass, on a bonfire site or tree stump; the apparent facts relating to the fungus – if it is a single example, one of a close group, or if specimens are scattered widely.

Note should also be made of the fungi's type, if known; the shape of cap and stem; presence or absence of a ring on the stem, or of a volva; the texture and colour of the cap and stem surfaces; the type, texture and colour of the gills and the flesh; whether the specimen is woody, juicy or odorous; height of stem; area of cap; whether any young specimens present have veils. Also relevant are the more abstract details of date, time of day, and weather conditions – and a reminder to note the fungoid aroma when on the habitat, since this may be a characteristic for easy identification which could be lost – the odour emitted in a room several hours later could be totally different.

A final mention should be made of whether the fungus changes colour by bruising or handling.

To facilitate reference, the same order should be followed for every specimen: the writer's order is offered as a suggestion.

If at all possible, a fungus should be represented by specimens in several stages of growth, since some species differ so much in youth and age that identification is again hazarded.

The mycologist who is able to take colour pictures or transparencies of the fungi in their natural habitat will add appreciably to the merit of his collection, as will the collector who is sufficiently skilled to make pencil or pastel colour sketches – which should not prove too difficult since drawing a fungus does not call for the finesse of an artist.

Some colour representation is beneficial since a number of fungi change colour on preservation. In later years the mycologist will be surprised how useful his illustrations can be as memory-joggers, particularly if his colour photos also incorporate an idea of scale – a ruler or coin – and the relevant page from a small, bold-printed calendar.

Further optional equipment must include a strong magnifying glass for on-site inspections, and hopefully a good home microscope for detailed examination, in particular of spores: there are indeed occasions on which microscopic study is the only sure way to distinguish between species, and it is invaluable for the study of rusts and smuts.

As part of the collection and for reference, especially for identification of difficult or unknown specimens, spore-prints will also prove beneficial to record the spore colour and the pattern of the gills. In most instances that follow, the spore colour is given for that final proof of identification should all else fail or be inconclusive, though it should be noted that in some instances, for example the white group, the spores may in fact be creamy or a very pale yellow. There are also variations of browns and pinks.

To make a spore-print the stem must be cut off close to the cap and laid gills downward on a sheet of white paper or cellophane where it should remain undisturbed for several hours, preferably overnight.

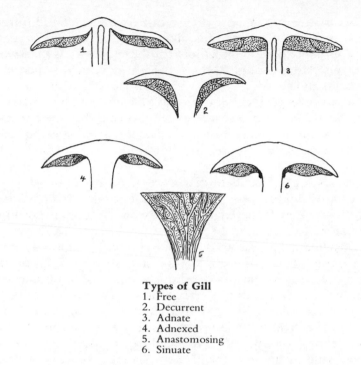

Types of Gill
1. Free
2. Decurrent
3. Adnate
4. Adnexed
5. Anastomosing
6. Sinuate

The cap must then be lifted off, carefully, while not allowing the slightest breath or draught to disturb the spores, when on the paper should be seen an exact print of the gills, indicating all their characteristics. This spore-print should now be sprayed very carefully with lacquer or a fixative; as an added protection it can also be covered with a sheet of clear plastic and taped around the edges. Fungus collectors in the past used to prepare their spore prints by laying the cap gills downward on a weakly gummed piece of paper so the shed spores were fixed to the gum. Disadvantages to this method were that the fragile gills would also become attached and after a period of time the gum tended to discolour the print.

If the operation is being conducted in a warm room, which may cause distortion or too quick drying of the specimen, a simple expedient is the placing of a larger glass container over the whole process.

A variation of the spore print is called for when one does not wish to remove the fungi's stem: here, a sheet of paper – appropriately coloured to allow for the spores – has a hole cut in it just large enough to take the stem, which is then slid through and stood, carefully, in a jam jar so that the paper is once more level. Dehydration can be countered by putting a little water in the jar, as well as by covering the entire work, and it is a factor that must be considered since some species will not eject their spores if the humidity is not sufficiently high.

Spores for independent microscopic examination can also be collected in this way, but should not be taken from a print; neither are they laquered, but can be stored in a small envelope or plastic bag.

Despite all precautions, one may still experience disappointment in not having a satisfactory print. There are many reasons for this, beyond the question of humidity: the cap may be too old or not yet mature, or the paper may be of the wrong colour. Since spores come in a range of colours within the creams, yellows, pinks, browns and purples, as well as black or white, the choice of paper colour is critical. A good rule-of-thumb would be to make spore prints of white-gilled fungi on black paper, and those with coloured gills on white paper.

The preservation of some of the fungi themselves, also presents problems. While the tough, woody specimens like the Bracket Fungi retain their form and colour fairly well through the drying process, the fleshy specimens are more likely to change.

Drying, ideally, should be rapid, and with a flow of air at about 40°C, either from a fan heater direct, or in the thermal from an electric fire (never in the direct radiant heat) or a 60 watt bulb or bunsen burner under a perforated biscuit tin.

Fair results can also be obtained in a cooling oven, over the ashes of a dying fire, or on a plate rack if there is no rising steam. An airing cupboard may be used, or even the sun itself through the medium of a greenhouse or conservatory – direct solar drying is rare in Britain, being more suitable for southern parts of North America.

Some specimens, notably the larger Agarics, may have to be cut in half to facilitate drying.

Another method of preservation is freeze drying; though it is very successful in retaining both shape and colour it does, however, require rather elaborate equipment. The method was excellently detailed by Mr D. A. L. Davies in his paper, 'The Preservation of Larger Fungi by Freeze–Drying', published in the *Transactions of the British Mycological Society*, Vol. 45, 1962, which I quote:

'APPARATUS: The equipment required is very simple (though cumbersome), and the items are to be found in most laboratories. Specimens have usually been frozen in a deep-freeze conservator of commercial design (Kelvinator) running at $-20°C$. Alternatively, adequate freezing conditions can be obtained with solid CO_2 ("Drikold") in acetone or ethanol. A satisfactory vacuum can be obtained with a rotary oil pump; a "Speedivac" (Edwards 2S 50) has generally been used. The pump should be in such condition as to maintain a pressure below $0·01$ mm. Hg in the system and should be fitted with an anti suck–back valve in case of power failure, and with a water trap (P_2O_5). Pyrex desiccators (12 in. diam.) have been used; several of these may be evacuated with one pump. Each desiccator contains a gauze–covered reservoir, holding about 300 ml. of commercial grade conc. H_2SO_4. Glass crystallizing dishes (8 in. diam.), in which the specimens have been frozen, fit conveniently over the gauze, space being left between gauze and dish to allow free access of water vapour to the desiccant. Good rubber pressure tubing and silicone vacuum grease are required to maintain a satisfactory vacuum.

'METHOD: In the present system specimens are frozen and rapidly transferred to desiccators where a high vacuum is immediately applied. The ice vaporizes and the vapour is absorbed by the H_2SO_4; the non–volatile matter (the whole structural part of the toadstool in this case) is left intact in the dry state. Melting is prevented by the cooling which results from rapid vaporization. Since fungi generally grow in damp places and are not provided with protection against water loss, there is no interference with the egress of water vapour. The speed of drying depends on the difference between the vapour pressure of ice at the temperature of the specimen (0·77 mm. Hg at −20°C.) and that remaining in the system after applying the vacuum pump.

'Preparation of Specimens: Specimens are distributed in crystallizing dishes and left at −20°C. overnight to freeze; they may be kept indefinitely at this temperature. Actually a few hours is sufficient to freeze small specimens. It is convenient to group large and small specimens in separate dishes since the duration of drying depends on the maximum thickness of the largest specimen in a batch. Those weighing 100 g. or more should be weighed before freezing because it is necessary to check later that they have dried to constant weight. For smaller specimens a little experience enables one to judge the time for complete drying.

'For certain types of agaric, e.g., those red hygrophori which blacken when touched, the relatively large ice crystals which form on slow freezing will damage the cells to some extent and produce a slight blackening. Better results can be obtained by very rapid freezing to produce much smaller ice crystals. This can be achieved by dropping them into some (preferably water-immiscible) solvent in equilibrium with solid CO_2, e.g. chloroform at −70°C. The specimen can thereafter be touched only with well cooled forceps (to avoid local melting and damage) and should be freed from adhering solvent by quickly drying in a desiccator evacuated with a water pump before warming again to −20°C. Specimens which have a glutinous covering of mucopolysaccharide (e.g. *Oudemansiella mucida, Gomphidius* spp. etc.) dry satisfactorily in the usual way, but on re-exposure to the air the glutinous layer absorbs moisture, shrinks and crinkles the surface of the pileus. If this crinkling is not required (to indicate that the specimen was originally glutinous) the substance should be washed off before freezing, because there is no satisfactory chemical or enzymic method of degrading these substances without doing further damage. With large specimens, it is often convenient to split the stem longitudinally to at least half of its thickness, as this will reduce the drying time by half; this is recommended particularly for those with a large "bulb". For some of the species with long thin fragile stems it is desirable to insert a wire through the length of the stem before freezing, to reduce liability to breakage after drying.

'Drying: Dishes of frozen specimens should be transferred very rapidly to desiccators and the vacuum applied immediately. Specimens cannot be handled in the frozen state without leaving a blemish on the dry product. A little experience enables one to judge the drying time for most specimens; small ones (*Mycena* and the like) take a few hours, medium-sized (*Russula*, etc.) 2-3 days, and the largest, e.g. *Amanita*, up to a week. It is essential to dry large ones to constant weight since a gram (or less) of ice remaining in the centre of the thickest part will melt on re-exposure to the air and ruin the specimen by local distortion. Since a dry agaric is a good heat insulator and drying is progressive from the outside, a partly dry specimen can safely be removed for weighing and be replaced in the vacuum for further drying until no further weight loss can be detected. During the first few hours of drying, or the first day for the larger kinds, the rate at which water vapour is removed is very high on account of the very large exposed surface area, especially when the gills are drying out. At this time the rate of diffusion of water through the H_2SO_4 may be too slow, resulting in a layer of water forming over the acid. This will be followed by an accumulation of water vapour, slowing of evaporation and a rise of temperature of the specimen to melting point. This danger is indicated by the arrival of water vapour in the P_2O_5 trap on the pump. It is therefore necessary to stir the acid in the reservoir by a circular motion of the desiccator on the bench; this can be facilitated by placing a few glass marbles beforehand in the acid reservoir. Alternatively, desiccators may be placed on magnetic stirrers, a polythene covered magnet having been placed in the acid beforehand. For specimens (or batches) weighing 300 g. or more it should be borne in mind that the amount of H_2SO_4 conveniently held in a reservoir (about 300 ml.) is sufficient to absorb about an equal volume of water only; a change of acid will then be necessary after 1 or 2 days of drying and specimens should be replaced at $-20°C$. during this process. It has been found convenient to keep the desiccators and pump in a cold room (at 2-3°C.) in which the $-20°$ cabinet is kept. This is not

39

essential however. Drying has been carried out in desiccators kept at room temperature and very successful runs have also been made in the freeze-drying apparatus (Type 3) described by Record & Taylor (1958) ["Freeze-drying equipment for large-scale laboratory use", *Biochem. Jl.*, 68]. In this case the spinner and heater were not used but the capacity to condense up to 30 l. of water is a helpful feature. In these very large metal desiccators kept at room temperature it takes much longer to reach a "drying" vacuum but, nevertheless, pre-frozen toadstools have not melted.

'Results and discussion: The best results are obtained with good fresh specimens, which should, however, be identified before drying because some diagnostic characters are lost, e.g. smell, taste, texture and colour changes of tissues and fluids. On the other hand it seems likely that some characters of the freeze-dried material may prove to be of diagnostic value. Dried specimens have not suffered visible deterioration on storage in a normal laboratory atmosphere for seven years. Most agarics lose between 88 and 92% of their original weight on drying completely and generally regain 2-3% of their dry weight on re-exposure to a normal laboratory atmosphere. With only 10% of structural material, the products are naturally somewhat fragile but while some are more fragile than fresh specimens, many are markedly tougher. Overall shrinkage on drying averages about 10%; in large species the internal stresses of shrinkage sometimes causes cracks in the pileus. Where the pileus is naturally easily separable from the stem, this is also true of the dried product and a wire inserted before drying is helpful. Preservation of colour is generally very good, e.g. reds of *Amanita, Russula, Hygrophorus*; greens, e.g. *Stropharia aeruginosa*; blue of *Leptonia*; purples of *Tricholoma* etc. Hygrophanous species dry to their palest form, indeed all species whose colour has a component which is a structural enhancement of slight pigmentation dry very pale. In a few instances colour may be obscured by a glutinous covering drying white over the surface, e.g. *Boletus elegans.* Only the yellows of *Clavaria* appear to fade rather quickly on storage. One anomaly encountered is that several species of *Agaricus* become uniformly yellow in addition to *A. xanthodermus.* The quality of preservation generally, however,

40

is such that a series of *Coprinus* can be made to show the successive stages of autolysis and these do not change on storage. Fungi having a jelly–like consistency, e.g. *Auricularia* and *Tremella*, present no problem and it is a pleasure to record that the slight residual smell of *Phallus impudicus* is not unlike that of hyacinths. In the course of drying the community of parasites housed within specimens is killed, so that the products are largely sterilized. A small survival rate would be expected for bacteria and micro–fungi but these present no further problem if specimens are stored in a reasonably dry atmosphere. Mites have been kept at bay with *p*–dichloroben-zene.'

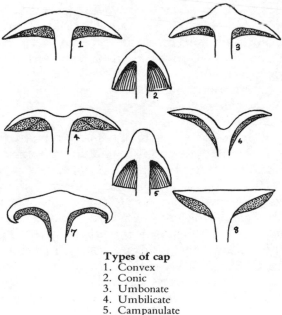

Types of cap
1. Convex
2. Conic
3. Umbonate
4. Umbilicate
5. Campanulate
6. Funnel
7. Involute
8. Plane

Whichever method of preservation is used, the best chances lie with drying the specimens as soon as possible after collecting them. Mycologists living in an area with high atmospheric humidity should store their specimens either in a desiccator over calcium chloride or in sealed polythene bags with a few granules of silica gel. Either of these methods prevents the specimens being ruined by moulds.

In drying, the microscopic characters of fungi are also preserved but in some instances may be shrunken. These can be restored to their usual appearance and size by warming a small piece of the tissue in water prior to examination. Another method is to mount the tissue in 10 per cent ammonia solution or 1 to 2 per cent potassium hydroxide.

A third method of preserving is to place the fungi in jars of alcohol. This has an advantage with those species that are difficult to air – or freeze–dry, or, like *Phallus*, are strongly odorous, but an obvious disadvantage with a large collection would be the amount of room space needed to store the jars, even if they each contained several species.

There are still more methods. One, using an old recipe, is quoted below without comment:

'Take two ounces of sulphate of copper, or blue vitriol, and reduce it to powder; pour upon it a pint of boiling water; and when cold add half a pint of spirits of wine; cork it well, and call it "the pickle". To eight pints of water add one and a half pints of spirits of wine, and call it "the liquor". Be provided with a number of wide-mouthed bottles of different sizes, all well fitted with corks. The fungi should be left on the table as long as possible, to allow the moisture to evaporate; they should then be placed in the pickle for three hours, or longer if necessary; after which they should be placed in the bottles intended for their reception, which are then filled with the liquor and well corked and sealed.'

Yet another method is by pressing thin sections, much as one would press a flower or leaf. The section must be taken very carefully, using a one-sided razor blade, and dried between sheets of blotting paper, which may need to be changed several times for the larger, more fleshy types. It should be possible to take samples which incorporate the gill section, the ring, and the volva, all in perfect preservation.

The final option is one described by T. A. Coward in his book, *Life of the Wayside and Woodland* (Warne): 'Several fungi of each species should be used. From one the skin of the cap is stripped and half the skin of the stalk; this is then fastened to the sheet to look like the living fungus. Another specimen is cut in section, showing the attachment of the gills, and a spore-print of the cap is added.' Although some of the method is practicable, the average collector would require extreme skill to strip the skin of the cap from some of the species and it would have to be attempted when the cap is at the right degree of maturity to avoid fragmenting.

How the collector stores his specimens depends largely on his circumstances and the space available, but a satisfactory way is by attaching the fungus – the dried cap and stem, or the pressed section – with its relevant spore prints, to a sheet of suitably coloured card with the use of transparent adhesive tape, and filing it carefully in a suitably large envelope.

An alternative method is to wrap the cap and stem separately in tissue, with a piece of card backing, and then store them in envelopes. As adhesive tape has a tendency to yellow with age it is advisable to place transparent plastic sheeting or cellophane over the fungi and attach the tape to this and the card, rather than tape directly on to the fungi. If this is done in the long-term if the tape yellows the plastic and tape can easily be replaced.

However the specimens are stored it is necessary to put some naphthalene or 'para' crystals in packets and place one in each of the larger envelopes. If the specimens are wrapped in tissue the dehydrant crystals can be placed loose in the envelopes. Finally, some naphthalene crystals should be scattered on the bottom of the filing cabinet drawers, or mothballs put in the corners, to prevent the specimens being damaged by fungus beetles or other insects.

In either of the methods a label, written in Indian ink or waterproof ink, should be stuck to a top corner of the envelope, giving the English name, scientific name and family of the fungus.

In each envelope should be a card with a copy of the vital

data recorded at the time of collection, to support which the mycologist should maintain another, more comprehensive record book covering everything that is known about every fungus in the collection – and here, too, further colour prints or paintings could find a ready home.

The collector may, however, feel that a card index system, with its scope for expansion, is preferable to a rigid book: he should still record as much detail as is possible.

How the packaged specimens are stored is again a personal choice: initially, numerical or alphabetical order may be preferred; later the collector may make an arrangement by family, genus, class and sub-class, giving each specimen a reference to find it from the master record. The only considerations should be for ease of access, and adequate protection of the specimens from damage, whether by human accidental agency, or by insects.

Possessing the knowledge of the equipment needed, and of how to collect, preserve and store his fungi, the collector's next requirement is to know where to look in order to find his specimens. The beginner can start in his own garden, and the town or city plot can be as prolific in this respect as a rural half-rood. A lawn that is not too frequently mown or has corners or edges which are rarely trimmed, is the site where a number of grass-inhabiting species will occur. Living fruit trees and ornamentals may have certain fungi on their trunks, and an old tree stump or a reclining log of a fallen tree will almost certainly yield further examples. Fungi will also grow on the bottoms of stacked sawn logwood and on gate and fence posts, while other species can be found on bonfire sites, compost heaps, and ground where stable or farmyard manure has been standing.

Outside the collector's own garden, the type and number of fungi to be found will depend very much on the locality. As will be seen in the Habitats Aid to Identification, fungi are present in a variety of places: woodlands, meadows, wayside banks; on downland turf or marshy ground; on sand dunes, industrial tips from factories and mills, and sawdust heaps at sawmills. In fact, it is safe to say that the collector is certainly within range of several of these types of habitat and so will definitely find a variety of species. The serious collector will study his region in detail to know what he is likely to find – and what he is not. For example, woodlands contain the largest number of fungi, and sand dunes and swampy places the fewest, these latter being the specialists. It must also be remembered that species which occur in coniferous woodlands probably will not be found in broadleafed plantations. Some fungi flourish in beechlands but not in oak, while on the other hand there are species which can be found on the floor of both types of woodland. Such factors must be borne in mind when identifying fungi, and may be crucial in proving the identity of a specimen. Having a clear knowledge of what is likely to occur pays rewards in not wasting time on an excursion searching for a species that cannot possibly be in the area.

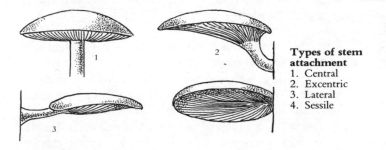

Types of stem attachment
1. Central
2. Excentric
3. Lateral
4. Sessile

Every month sees some fungus species growing, so the collector has the opportunity to continue his search without a break, the 'closed season' being confined to periods of severe frost which fungi cannot endure. However, some of the species which thrive on fallen or unhealthy timber are more tolerant to lower temperatures and can be found in the winter months. When it is mild some of the autumn species will continue into winter and equally when spring is mild some of the April and May species will appear earlier in the season. The most prolific period, however, is from the end of summer into late autumn.

With their numbers also largely governed by the rainfall, during spells of dry weather few of the expected species may be in evidence, development being delayed until the rains. Thus mycologists are among the few people who could benefit from a wet summer! Annoying as it is to farmers and holidaymakers alike, a wet harvest in August can bring forth species normally found in September and even October.

The collector who has done his research will know approximately where the species he wants to obtain are likely to occur. Should these be on open or accessible sites where the public is allowed, then there is no problem. But fungi also grow on private land, particularly woodlands from which the public is excluded. In these instances the prudent mycologist with an eye to future visits will first seek permission to enter, preferably in writing: he may find the landowner sufficiently interested to lead him to the best locations!

The mycologist, be he on private or public land, should also avoid litter, nor should he hack at trees nor leave open excavations and trampled vegetation. While he may escape reproach, the next student of fungi may find things entirely different.

Lastly, the collector will benefit considerably by becoming a member of his area's local natural history society, which may have a mycology section. Not only will its published literature be useful and contact be beneficial with other people interested in the same subjects, but the fungus-hunting excursions which are held from time to time are often to sites usually closed to the general public, permission being granted only to responsible members of nature societies and clubs. These excursions can also provide the student of fungi with the opportunity to see, if not on such occasions to collect, the rarer species with which this land of ours is remarkably well endowed.

3 Fungus Examples

BASIDIOMYCETES – Gasteromycetes

The *Gasteromycetes* group of the *Basidiomycetes*, which have their fruiting layers – the basidia and spores they produce – enclosed in the peridium until the spores are ripe for dispersal are divided into four orders: the *Phallales*, the *Lycoperdales*, the *Sclerodermales* and *Nidulariales*.

PHALLALES

The *Phallales* – the Stinkhorns have, in their mature form, a conical cap on a sterile stalk, and appear to grow from the cup-shaped volva. Because of their shape and smell they are easily detected and identified.

Collared Stinkhorn *(Dictyophora duplicata):*
North America, West Europe, England.
   Woodlands and forests; on dead leaves. Singly or scattered. Common, North America; rare, England, Europe. Summer.
   Similar in shape to Common Stinkhorn, but has a prominent, net-like indusium hanging inside the conical cap. The indusium – the outer case of the spore cluster – is believed to make the fungus more conspicuous after dusk and attract night-flying insects to its spore-mass. The sponge-like stem has a bulbous volva at its base. Supposedly poisonous.
Colour: cap, white, covered by greenish-brown slime; indusium collarette, white or rosy-white; stem, whitish; volva, greyish-white.
Height: up to 7 inches; indusium several inches in length.

Columnar Stinkhorn *(Clathrus columnatus):*
North America.
   Gardens, woodland areas; on grass and dead leaves. Singly. Fairly common. Summer.

Similar to Lattice Stinkhorn, but with up to five curved, spongy columns that join at their summit to form an oval network; the viscous spore masses are sited on the inner sides of the columns. Poisonous. Has the typical foetid aroma.
Colour: spore-mass olive-brown; columns pinkish-red or cinnabar-red.
Height: up to 5 inches; up to 3 inches in diameter.

Common Stinkhorn, wood witch (*Phallus impudicus*)

Collared Stinkhorn
(*Dictyophora duplicata*)

Common Stinkhorn, Wood Witch *(Phallus impudicus):*
British Isles, North America.

Woodlands, wooded gardens; on dead leaves. Singly or scattered examples. Common. Summer, late autumn.

The immature rounded white sporophore, the 'egg', up to 2 inches in length, develops just below the surface of the habitat; the white mycelium is branched, cord-like. On dissecting an immature specimen one can see the compressed white core which will develop into the stem, surrounded by the blackish-olive gleba. The peridium has thin, white inner and outer membranes and a thick, soft, gelatinous middle layer. As soon as the spores are ripe the 'egg' is pierced at the top of the peridium by the expanding stem, with the gleba on its cap, the peridium remaining as the cup-like volva at the base. This expansion is rapid, sometimes taking as little as one and a half hours.

The mature stem is erect or slightly curved, sponge-like and hollow; the cap, covered by the gleba, is conical, with noxious smelling olive-green or blackish-olive slime. Flies are attracted to the strong unpleasant odour and achieving spore distribution by eating the spore mass, leaving only the white honeycomb network. The 'egg' is edible; the mature fungus supposedly poisonous, but certainly unpalatable; a nuisance when growing near houses due to its aroma.
Colour: white cap covered at first by olive-green or blackish-olive slime; stem white; volva brownish or whitish.
Height: up to 8 inches; approximately 1 inch thick.

Dog Stinkhorn *(Mutinus caninus):*
British Isles, North America.

Woodlands; among old, damp leaves, on old stumps, rotting wood. Singly. Common. Summer, autumn.

Develops from an oval, white or yellowish 'egg', up to 1 inch in length, with white mycelium cords, and is the familiar Stinkhorn shape, but smaller; stem slender and hollow, with a porous, pitted wall; cap adnate to the stem and not distinct from it; small volva, rounded at base. Has only a slight foetid aroma.
Colour: cap orange-red or red, covered at first by the dark

49

green or greenish-black slimy spore-mass; stem whitish, pinkish, pinkish-buff or orange; volva greyish-white. Height: up to 4 inches.

Dog Stinkhorn *(Mutinus caninus)*

Lattice Stinkhorn *(Clathrus ruber [cancellatus]):*
North America, southern and south-west British Isles, Isle of Wight, Scilly Isles, southern Europe.

Gardens, on hedge-banks, occasionally woodland edges; on dead leaves and undisturbed soil. Singly or several. Common North America, fairly common British Isles, common southern Europe; especially favours warm habitats. Summer.

Similar to the Common, Collared and Dog Stinkhorns, it develops from a reticulated 'egg' which is eventually burst by the mature fungus to form an open latticed receptacle, the

remains of the peridium forming an irregular cup at the base. The inner surface of the branches of the lattice bears a slimy gleba. Supposedly poisonous. Has a powerful foetid aroma. Colour: lattice red above, pink below or entire coral pink, vermillion, or pinkish-red; gleba olive-green or olive-brown; peridium cup white.
Height: up to 5 inches; up to 7 inches in diameter.

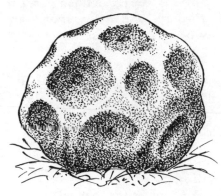

Lattice Stinkhorn *(Clathrus ruber [cancellatus])*

LYCOPERDALES

The *Lycoperdales* – Puffballs and Earth Stars – when mature have a powdery gleba with the capillitium threads attached to the inner layer of the peridium, except in *Bovista*. Both types are easily recognized by their shape.

LYCOPERDACEAE

Puffballs are both common and familiar, though there are many variations within the species. They are found in different sizes, shapes, and structures; their spores differ, as do the capillitium, and the method by which the rupturing peridia release their spores. The mycelium cords are white.

Puffballs are edible when young and the flesh is white and cheesy, but on maturing it yellows and finally turns brown and inedible. The name is apt, the spores being emitted like puffs of smoke from the single pore at the top when the

51

mature sporophore is suddenly squeezed. In nature, rain has the same effect and helps to distribute the spores. The family is divided into three genera – the *Lycoperdon*, the *Bovista* and the *Calvatia*.

LYCOPERDON

These differ from *Calvatia* by having clearly defined pores at the apex of the peridium, through which the spores are released. The peridium has two layers, but the fragile outer layer at first ornamented with warts or spines, soon disintegrates and disappears. The spores are spherical. The capillitium are attached either to the endoperidium or the sterile tissue of the columella.

Beautiful Puffball *(Lycoperdon pulcherrimum):*
North America.
   Gardens, woodlands, waste places; on soil. Singly, not colonial. Fairly common. Summer.
   The sporophore has stem-like base or is spherical. Young specimens have an exoperidium adorned with tapered spines; on maturing, those at the base become darker while the upper spines are shed. Edible.
Colour: young; spines greenish-white on exoperidium, mature exoperidium silver-grey.
Height: up to 2 inches; diameter the same.

Common Puffball (British Isles), Gemmed Puffball (North America), Gem-Studded Puffball (North America) *(Lycoperdon [gemmatum] perlatum):*
British Isles, North America.
   Meadows, gardens, golf courses and similar grassy places; on earth, decaying wood, the latter sometimes in open woodlands. Colonial. Very common. Summer, autumn.
   In one strain, the sporophore is pear-shaped, with the fertile upper portion being quite small; another strain is top-shaped, with the sterile base of the sporophore being the smaller. In both, the mycelium cords are white. Young specimens have an outer layer with erect, tapering and fragile spines, surrounded by a ring of small warts; these warts and spines

decreasing in size down the fungus until on the base are only scurfy granules. The long spines fall off first, followed by the shorter ones, leaving spots, short pointed warts and a network of irregular scars. Edible, if flesh white and firm.

Colour: sporophore snow-white when young, becoming creamy-yellowish, greyish, tan or brown when mature; gleba white, greenish-yellow, becoming olive-brown; spores olive-brown.

Height: up to 4 inches; up to 2½ inches in diameter.

Common Puffball, Gemmed Puffball, Gem-Studded Puffball *(Lycoperdon [gemmatum] perlatum)*

Lycoperdon Hiemale *(Depressum):*
British Isles.

Grassland. Colonial. Common. Summer, autumn, winter.

The sporophore top-shaped, the fertile upper portion narrowing to a short, solid stem. The contracted sterile base sometimes accounts for half the total height and is separated from the gleba by a distinct skin. Immature specimens are covered with large and small spines and powdery, granular scales which fall as the fungus matures, leaving a smooth surface. The mouth is large and situated at the apex.

Colour: young yellowish-white, dull yellow, then yellowish-brown; spores olive-green.
Height: up to 2½ inches; diameter the same.

Lycoperdon Hiemale *(Depressum)*

Spiny Puffball *(Lycoperdon echinatum):*
British Isles, North America.
   Woodlands, particularly beech; on dead leaves and earth. Not common. Summer, autumn.

Spiny Puffball *(Lycoperdon echinatum)*

The sporophore has a rounded upper portion with the base stem-like; it has a mass of long, pointed spines surrounded by small warts on a patterned outer skin. Edible when young.

Colour: sporophore brown; spines dark brown or purplish-brown, probably only dark brown at their tips; gleba yellowish then purple-brown; spores purple-brown.

Height: up to 2½ inches; up to 1½ inches in diameter.

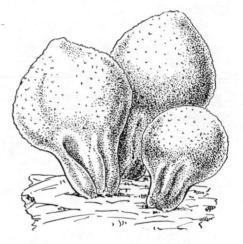

Stump Puffball, Pear-Shaped Puffball *(Lycoperdon pyriforme)*

Stump Puffball (British Isles), Pear-Shaped Puffball (North America) *(Lycoperdon pyriforme):*

British Isles, North America.

On old decaying tree and fence stumps, the only British Puffball species to do so. Usually colonial, in crowded clusters. Common, Late summer, autumn, winter.

The pear-shaped sporophore has a stem which tapers to the base; has minute scaly warts, spines and granules which quickly disappear as it matures, leaving a flaccid smooth surface. Has an aroma claimed to be like fresh herrings.

Colour: young mealy-white; mature brown or brownish-grey when granules removed; mycelium cords white.

Height: up to 2 inches; diameter the same.

BOVISTA

These differ from the *Lycoperdon* in that the capillitium are free, with long, forking branches, there being no sterile base. The outer layer of the peridium is paper-like and flakes away to expose the thin, tough, shiny endoperidium. Another difference is that the endoperidium's mouth appears torn and irregular.

Small Round Puffball *(Bovista nigrescens)*:
British Isles.
   All types of grassland. Singly or scattered. Common. Throughout year.

Small Round Puffball *(Bovista nigrescens)*

The sporophore is rounded when young, but the outer layer breaks away to reveal the inner layer, when the fungus becomes more flattened; when mature, the endoperidium is irregular with jagged tears. At this stage the fungus may be uprooted and rolled along by the wind, so dispersing the ripe spores. Edible when young.
Colour: young, white or whitish-brown, inner layer greyish-white; mature purplish-brown, sometimes blackish; gleba purple; spores purplish-brown.
Spherical, up to $2\frac{1}{4}$ inches across.

Bovista plumbea:

British Isles.

Grassland, pastures, meadows, golf courses and similar. Common. Late summer, autumn.

Similar to *Bovista nigrescens*, but the endoperidium has a smaller split through which the spores escape. When mature the fungus may be uprooted and windblown to disperse the ripe spores. Edible when young.

Colour: young whitish-grey, inner layer whitish-grey; mature lead-grey; gleba purplish-brown; spores olive-brown.

Height: up to 2 inches; diameter up to $2\frac{1}{4}$ inches.

Giant Puffball *(Calvatia gigantea)*
[Lycoperdon giganteum]

CALVATIA

Differs from *Lycoperdon* in that the apex of the peridium breaks away into irregular portions so the spores can be released.

Giant Puffball, Tête de Mort *(Calvatia gigantea,* North America: *Lycoperdon giganteum).*

57

British Isles, Europe, North America.

Among grass in pastures, meadows, orchards, golf courses, lawns, roadside, occasionally woodland grassy areas; on old compost heaps and accumulated decaying vegetation. Singly or in a group of several, occasionally in rings. Variably common, population fluctuates. Occasionally spring, usual late summer, early autumn. Its conspicuous size usually immediately identifies this as the largest fungus.

The sporophore begins as a sphere, changing to oval or pumpkin shaped as it matures; virtually stemless, the plicate base is attached to the habitat by thick mycelium strands. The young Puffball's skin is thin and downy, changing to the texture of white kid, then chamois, before splitting to reveal the thin, brittle inner layer which eventually flakes away and collapses, allowing the spores to escape.

This fungus produces immense numbers of globose, warted spores, a figure of seven thousand million being quoted for an average specimen, while a large Canadian Puffball had an estimated twenty thousand million.

Examples have been found in fields and mistaken for bleached human skulls, giving rise to the belief that the area had been a battlefield, and explaining the grisly French name, Tête de Mort. Dried Puffballs have also been found under house floors and been so mistaken for human remains that police investigations have resulted. The dried fungi also found a use in rural districts to staunch bleeding.

The fungus is edible when young and still white, having a firm, cheesy consistency, but once it is powdery and brown it is inedible.

Colour: young, white becoming creamy, yellowish-greenish, then on maturity to olive-brown; gleba olive; spores olive-brown.

Height: average 11 inches, by 12 inches diameter – from large turnip to football size being usual in British Isles, but the average North American Puffball is twice this size, weighing 30 lb. or more. But huge specimens have been discovered in both continents: one, 11 inches high and 49 in circumference weighed 10 lb. 2 ounces. Another discovered in New York State in 1877 and mistaken at a distance for a reclining sheep, was $9\frac{1}{2}$ inches in height, but at its largest diameter measured 5 feet 4 inches.

Mosaic Puffball *(Calvatia caelata [Lycoperdon caelatum]):* British Isles.

Grassy areas, pastures, downland. Common, northern Britain, less common southern Britain. Summer, autumn.

The sporophore is pear-shaped and tapering, with a flattened apex; it has a stem-like sterile base with a diaphragm separating it from the spore mass of the fertile upper portion. The exoperidium cracks into hexagonal areas with raised warts which subsequently fall off. The inner layer thus exposed flakes away at its thin apex to allow the spores to escape, after which the inverted pear shaped sterile base and lower portion of the torn peridium survive as an irregular, goblet-shaped entity which may be wind-blown for several months. Edible when young.

Colour: young white or greyish-white, becoming yellowish or grey, then brownish; spores dark olive.

Height: up to 6 inches; up to 7 inches in diameter.

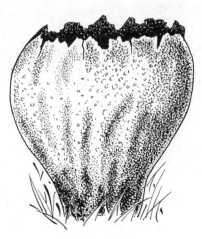

Mosaic Puffball *(Calvatia caelata [Lycoperdon caelatum])*

GEASTRACEAE

The Earth Stars, related to the Puffballs, are not very common but are quickly recognized by their characteristic shapes. The thick outer wall has three layers and when mature splits from the apex down to just below the centre line to give up to 14 pointed lobes or rays which fold back to form a star-shaped base.

The thin inner wall, thus exposed, appears like a small, rounded Puffball, erect and prominent on its base. This endoperidium, equipped with a pore mouth at its apex, also has many-branching capillitium and a central columella. A further distinguishing characteristic, if one were needed, is that the mycelium is sometimes above the habitat surface – usually sand – and entangled in the exoperidium lobes.

Crowned Earth Star
(Geastrum coronatus)

Crowned Earth Star *(Geastrum coronatus):*
British Isles, North America.

Woodlands on earth, particularly among pine needles. Singly or in colonies. Uncommon. Summer, autumn.

The exoperidium splits into up to 8 lobes which are sometimes so curved that they lift the fungus from the ground. The endoperidium has a ridge around the projected apical pore.
Colour: brown.
Height and diameter: up to 2 inches.

60

Earth Star, Triplex Earth Star (North America)
(Geastrum triplex):
British Isles, North America.

Woodlands, especially beech woodlands. Fairly common, moreso southern England. Summer, autumn.

The mature exoperidium splits into 6 to 8 unequal lobes with long pointed tips which either lie flat or turn under the fruit body to form an arched base; when young it is shaped like an onion. It is identified by the thick fleshy collar around the base of the mature endoperidium, and the raised apical pore fringed with fine silky hairs.

Colour: endoperidium pale brown, sometimes pale pink or flesh, darkening as it matures; collar yellowish becoming pinkish-brown; spores purplish-brown.

Height and diameter: up to 2 inches.

Earth Star, Triplex Earth Star *(Geastrum triplex)*

Geastrum fimbriatum:
British Isles.

Woodlands. Usually colonial. Fairly common. Summer, autumn.

The mature exoperidium splits into 6 to 9 unequal pointed lobes which either lie flat or turn under the fruit body, while the lower unsegmented portion forms a cup around the base of the sessile (stemless) endoperidium; the endoperidium forms a smooth, round bag, the apical pore being a fringed cone.

Colour: exoperidium pale buff or fawn; endoperidium pale brown; spores dark brown.

Height and diameter: up to 1½ inches.

Geastrum fornicatus:

British Isles.

In grass, sometimes on woodland edges. Usually colonial. Uncommon. Summer, autumn.

Exoperidium splits into two layers, the inner layer divided to form four or five lobes bent backwards and downwards and may be incurved, but erect lifting the fungi away from the habitat, the lobe tips being attached to four or five short lobes on the outer layer that forms a cup on the habitat; the endoperidium has an apophysis or ring-like swelling where joins short stalk, the apical pore or mouth being ciliate, conical, finally tubular.

Colour: exoperidium buff or brown, endoperidium dark brown.

Height: up to $2\frac{1}{2}$ inches; up to $2\frac{1}{2}$ inches in diameter.

SCLERODERMALES

The *Sclerodermales* – Earth Balls – are identified from the *Lycoperdales* – Puffballs – because they have only one firm, thick outer layer or peridium. There is no pore opening, at the top, the round spores, with spiny or network-like areas on the walls, being released when the upper peridium splits through weathering or decay. The coloured gleba is compact at first, becoming powdery. The following two species have their mycelium in the habitat, and have no capillitium. Each can be found as hosts of the parasitic *Boletus parasiticus*.

Common Earth Ball *(Scleroderma aurantium)*:

British Isles.

Woodlands, heaths, especially on sandy soil, also appears to have a preference for birch woods; on bare earth. Very common. Summer, autumn, early winter.

The sporophore is bun-shaped, flattened at the apex; base may be plicate; no stem. Flesh is marbled when immature, the peridium being thick and tough with large irregular scales. Poisonous when eaten in a sufficient quantity, although on the Continent it has been sold fraudulently as Truffles.

Colour: peridium interior whitish, becoming pinkish if cut; exterior pale brown with a yellow hue, or yellow-ochre; scales

brown; gleba greyish becoming purple-black with thin, whitish veins or tramal plates; spores purple-black.
Height: approaching 3 inches; width usually a little more.

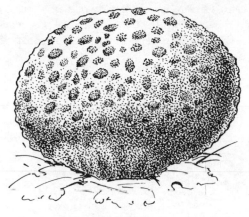

Common Earth Ball *(Scleroderma aurantium)*

Scleroderma verrucosum:
British Isles.

Woodlands, especially on rich soil. Common. Summer, autumn.

The bun-shaped sporophore has a slight stem, the base being lacunose; it is similar to the Common Earth Ball but the peridium's thin outer layer is smoother, the warts being small or absent.
Colour: peridium exterior dull greyish-brown or ochraceous when smooth; warts brown; gleba dark brown.
Height: approaching $2\frac{1}{2}$ inches; width slightly more.

NIDULARIA

The *Nidularia* sporophore is like a flattish cup, but the peridioles do not have the thread-like stalks attaching them to the wall of the peridium.

Nidularia pisiformis:
British Isles.

Woodlands, copses, wooded gardens and similar; on decaying leaves, sawdust and wood chips, twig debris, fallen rotting wood and branches. Not common. Throughout year.

The sporophore is at first near globular, becoming flat, rounded and hairy; the glossy peridioles are not attached but set in viscous mucus.

Colour: brown; peridioles brown.

Cup diameter: $\frac{3}{8}$ inch.

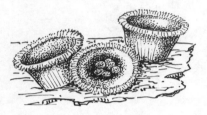

Nidularia pisiformis

Nidularia confluens:
British Isles.

Occurs in similar habitats to *Nidularia pisiformis*, sometimes in dense colonies so that some of the sporophores are deformed by overcrowding. Not common. Throughout year.

The sporophore is similar to that of *Nidularia pisiformis*; the peridium is thin with fine hairs, and the unattached peridioles are round and compressed.

Colour: peridium whitish; peridioles dark chestnut-brown.

Cup diameter: $\frac{3}{8}$ inch.

White Bird's Nest *(Nidularia candida)*:
North America.

On decaying wood, twigs, straw or sawdust. Singly or colonial. Fairly common. Summer, autumn.

Similar to *Nidularia pisiformis* (above), except for colour.

Colour: peridium exterior white, becoming darker as it matures; interior, yellowish.

Diameter: up to $\frac{3}{8}$ inch.

Plates 1, 2, 3, 4 Four stages of the **Dryad's Saddle** (*Polyporus [Melanopus] squamosus*), which occurs on stumps and trunks of dead deciduous trees, especially elm and ash, in late spring, summer and early autumn.
(1) *above*, Shows a very early stage in development.

(2) *below*, A young specimen.

(3) *above*, An upper view of the saddle-shaped bracket showing the scales in approximate concentric rings.

(4) *below*, A tier of overlapping mature Dryad's Saddle brackets on elm.

CRUCIBULUM

As the name implies, the *Crucibulum* sporophore is cup-shaped, the peridium comprising one layer of hyphae. The peridioles are attached to the inner wall of the peridium by a slender stalk or funiculus.

Common Bird's Nest *(Crucibulum vulgare):*
British Isles, North America.

Woodlands, wooded gardens or any site where appropriate decaying materials occur; on soil, dead twigs, wood, dead and decaying plant matter, rotting materials such as sacking. Singly or colonial. Common. Autumn, winter.

The sporophore is at first globular with a double wall; as it matures it becomes a bell-shaped cup with a flat, hairy, double-layered yellowish-brown membrane acting as a lid-covering; this breaks to expose the smooth interior with its circular peridioles and a nipple-like protuberance which is attached to the slender stalk or funiculus.

Colour: yhung, exterior cinnamon-brown, greying when mature; interior whitish or pale brown; peridioles dull whitish or pale brown.

Height and diameter: up to ½ inch.

Common Bird's Nest
(Crucibulum vulgare)

CYATHUS

The sporophore of *Cyathus* is cup-shaped, the peridium consisting of three layers of hyphae. The peridioles are also attached to the inner wall of the peridium by slender thread-like funiculi growing from the side of the peridiole in a shallow depression or umbilicus.

Striate Bird's Nest *(Cyathus striatus):*
British Isles, North America.

Woodlands, wooded gardens; on sticks, rotting stumps and fence posts, beechmast, conifer cones, decaying fern fronds and similar debris, occasionally on soil. Singly, but usually colonial, in dense groups. Common. Spring, summer, autumn.

Striate Bird's Nest *(Cyathus striatus)*

The broad, cup or bell-shaped sporophore is immediately identified by the neat longitudinal furrows on its glossy, cup interior. The outer surface is hairy with incurved edges. A membrane later breaks to expose the interior with its circular, flattened peridioles rather like split peas or lentils.
Colour: cup, exterior reddish-brown; interior grey; peridioles whitish.
Height: approximately ½ inch; diameter, ⅜ inch.

Cyathus olla:
British Isles.

Gardens and habitats similar to Striate Bird's Nest; frequently on soil. Common.

The sporophore is similar to that of Striate Bird's Nest; a broad cup shape resembling an inverted bell tapering to a narrow base, but smooth instead of fluted; the outer surface silky or smooth.
Colour: exterior grey; interior grey or brown; peridioles glossy, blackish, greyish or brown.
Height: approximately ½ inch; diameter ⅜ inch.

4 Fungus Examples

BASIDIOMYCETES – Hymenomycetes

The *Hymenomycetes* group of the *Basidiomycetes* have their *hymenium* or fruiting layer, the fertile basidia and the spores they produce, exposed to the air before the spores are ripe for dispersal. The *Hymenomycetes* are divided into seven orders – the *Agaricales* (*Leucosporae, Rhodosporae, Ochrosporae, Melanosporae*), the *Boletaceae*, the *Polyporaceae*, the *Hydnaceae*, the *Clavariaceae*, the *Thelephoraceae*, and *Meruliaceae*. Among them are some of our most familiar members of the Gill and Pore Fungi.

AGARICALES – LEUCOSPORAE

The *Agaricales* are fleshy, the sporophores being cap-shaped with the hymenia on distinct gills on the underside. The colour of the spores is used to place them into groups for quick identification, but this does not mean, for example, that all Agarics which produce white or pale spores are closely related, since other details must be considered in identifying the families to which the white or pale spore-producing fungi belong. The following groups are in this category of white-spored or pale-spored Agarics – the *Leucosporae* – *Amanitaceae, Lepiotae, Tricholomataceae, Pleurotaceae, Hygrophoraceae, Russulaceae, Cantharellaceae.*

AMANITACEAE
Amanita

The *Amanita* genus includes the very poisonous species responsible for the majority of fatalities and it is therefore vitally important to identify these with certainty during collection, either for study or for consumption: perhaps it is wiser to avoid those *Amanitas* which are edible as they can resemble poisonous species, thus avoiding the chance of incorrect identification. This genus is the most highly developed of the Gill Fungi and has in the button stage both a partial veil and a universal or general veil; remnants of the latter sometimes found on the cap as patches or 'warts', while the lower veil fragment or cup-like volva survives at the base of the stem, the partial veil on breaking becomes the ring on the stem.

It is worth remembering that only the *Amanitas* have both a ring and a volva, although the ring may be poorly developed and the volva almost buried. It is for this reason, to obtain the specimen in its entirety, that one should dig up fungi rather than pull them up by the stem. The cap of *Amanita*, with its free gills, also tends to break easily at its junction with the stem.

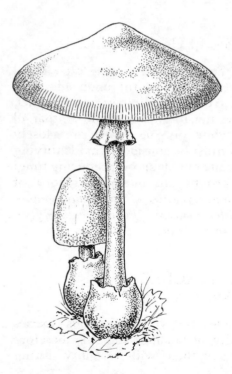

Caesar's Amanita
(Amanita caesarea)

Caesar's Amanita *(Amanita caesarea):*
North America, Europe, but not British Isles.

Open woodlands. Common. Autumn.

The cap is convex when young, becoming flatter, smooth and shiny when dry; striate on the margin. Gills are free, the stem smooth, with a ring towards the top similar to The Blusher. The cup-shaped volva is large, similar to that of the Destroying Angel. Edible.

Colour: cap orange-yellow; gills yellow; stem and ring pale orange-yellow; volva and spores white.

Height: up to 7 inches; cap up to 7 inches in diameter.

Death Cap
(Amanita phalloides)

Death Cap *(Amanita phalloides):*
British Isles, North America.

Deciduous woodlands, especially oak and beech, and adjoining grassland. Fairly common. Late summer, autumn.

The cap, rounded or oval when young, becoming convex

and then flat. Silky smooth when dry, slightly viscid or slimy when wet, perhaps with radiating fibrils on the upper surface, the cap is easy to peel. The gills are crowded and broad, varying in length; the stem is smooth with fine vertical lines on its upper portion, narrows from the swollen bulbous base to the cap, and may be hollow in old specimens. The ring is conspicuous though frail, radially striate on its upper stem and hanging down like a frill. The volva is cup-like and loose, with free edges. Very poisonous. Old decaying examples have a sweet, sickly aroma.

Colour: cap variable, yellowish–olive streaked with darker fibrils, but also yellowish-green, pale brown, buff, tan or white; flesh white, under cap skin flesh green or yellowish tint; gills white or cream, sometimes with a greenish tint; stem white or has a greenish tint; ring and spores white; volva white or yellowish.

Height: up to 5 inches; cap up to $3\frac{1}{2}$ inches in diameter.

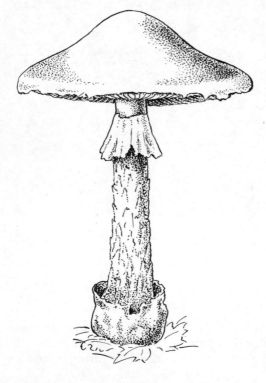

Destroying Angel
(*Amanita virosa*)

Destroying Angel *(Amanita virosa):*
British Isles, North America.

Damp mixed woodlands. Rare, British Isles. Summer, autumn.

The conical cap, slightly viscid, has similar characteristics to that of the Death Cap; the stem is rather slender and may be scaly. The silky ring is often irregular, incomplete, or lopsided, and may be partly attached to the cap rim. The volva is membranous, wide and free. Very poisonous.
Colour: cap pure white; gills white; stem white or marbled; ring and spores white.
Height: up to $7\frac{1}{2}$ inches; cap up to 5 inches in diameter.

False Death Cap, Bulbous Amanita *(Amanita citrina [mappa]):*
British Isles.

Mixed woodlands, especially beech. Very common. Late summer, early autumn.

False Death Cap, Bulbous Amanita
(Amanita citrina [mappa])

The cap is approximately convex and smooth, with several patches of the torn veil on its upper surface, but without the dark, fine radiating fibrils of Death Cap, with which it is often

71

confused despite its distinct differences. Important identification features are the different shape of the volva, in False Death Cap being short, sometimes completely separated from the stem and forming a distinct thick ridge around its bulbous base. The gills are narrow and crowded, free of or just touching the stem, which itself is smooth and slender with a tendency to hollowness. The ring, and the stem above it, are striate.

Harmless but unpalatable. When bruised the flesh has a strong aroma like raw potatoes, and a noxious flavour. The cap is easily peeled.

Colour: cap white or pale yellow, never greenish; veil patches white becoming yellowish or brownish; stem white or pale yellow; gills white, sometimes with yellowish edge; ring white above, yellowish below; volva white, yellowish or brownish.

Height: up to 4 inches; cap up to 3 inches in diameter.

Fly Agaric (British Isles), Fly Amanita (North America)
(Amanita muscaria):
British Isles, North America.

Open woodlands, especially under birch and conifer trees. Singly or in groups. Common. Late summer, autumn.

Immediately recognized as the fungus used by artists and craftsmen in children's picture books and toys, table decorations, and Disney films, as the seat or shelter for gnomes, elfs and fairies. The cap is rounded when young, then flattens with a striate or slightly upturned margin. Viscid when wet, it easily peels. The torn veil sometimes remains on the shiny upper surface of the cap as thick patches or warts, which may be arranged in a concentric pattern, but are sometimes absent on old specimens through being washed away by rain. The gills are crowded and free, but close to the stem; the stem, striate above the torn and hanging ring, is scaly, having narrowed from a bulbous base, the latter being the remnants of the volva in several concentric warty rings. The stem may hollow with maturity. Poisonous. So-named because it was originally used in milk as a fly killer.

Colour: conspicuous bright scarlet–red or orange–red, fading to yellowish; cap patches white or yellowish; gills white or

yellow tinted; stem white or yellowish; ring white above, yellowish below; volva white or yellowish; flesh white, yellowish under cap skin; spores white.
Height: up to 10 inches; cap up to 7 inches in diameter.

Fly Agaric, Fly Amanita *(Amanita muscaria)*

Fool's Mushroom, Spring Amanita (North America)
(Amanita verna):
British Isles, North America.

Woodlands, especially under beech trees. Rare, British Isles. Summer, early autumn, rarely spring. Cap similar to Death Cap with a slender stem and the membranous volva more sheath-like. Very poisonous.
Colour: entirely pure white, except that the cap centre may be tinted brownish.
Height: up to 5 inches; cap up to 3 inches in diameter.

**Fool's Mushroom,
Spring Amanita**
(Amanita verna)

Grey-Brown Amanita *(Amanita porphyria):*
North America.

Open coniferous woodlands, especially on clear tracks and paths. Singly or in groups. Common. Summer, late autumn.

The smooth cap, convex when young, flattens in maturity, with a slightly upturned rim and is viscid when wet; the torn veil may survive as a few small patches or 'warts' on the cap. The gills are crowded, unequal in length and free from the stem which narrows slightly from its bulbous base. The volva is membranous, its collar free from the stem and the large, membranous ring spreads downwards. May be harmless, but doubtful edibility.

Colour: cap grey-brown or pale brown, may have purplish tint; gills white or creamy; stem whitish, with streaky grey patterning; ring pale grey; volva greyish; flesh white; spores white.

Height: up to 5 inches; cap up to 4 inches in diameter.

Panther Cap (British Isles), False Blusher (British Isles), Panther Amanita (North America), Panther Agaric (North America) *(Amanita pantherina):*
British Isles, North America.

Deciduous woodlands, especially beech, open conifer forests, heaths, and pastures and lawns if close to coniferous woodland. Singly or in colonies. Fairly common, British Isles, common North America. Late spring, summer, late autumn; may continue into early winter if climate mild and moist.

Panther Cap, False Blusher, Panther Amanita, Panther Agaric *(Amanita pantherina)*

Similar to Fly Agaric, but smaller and with different colouring, it can also be mistaken for the edible Blusher (*Amanita rubescens*) though is itself very poisonous. The smooth cap flattens from its earlier convex shape and is shiny when dry but viscid when wet. Its margin is striate, with torn veil remains appearing as numerous small patches or warts sometimes pointed. The gills are crowded and narrow, but wider near the cap margin, and free; the smooth stem tapers gently from a slightly bulbous base, is striate above the centrally or lower centrally placed ring, and hollows with age. The ring itself is thin, lopsided, sometimes striate, and spreading downward. The volva remains membranous and adheres to the stem with up to three freestanding girdles. The fungus, which sometimes has a sickly aroma or smells of radishes, takes its name from its panther-like spots or warts. Colour: cap dull yellowish-brown, dull brown, tan, greyish-brown, with a darker centre; patches or warts white or cream; gills, stem, volva, ring and flesh always white; does not redden as in the Blusher; spores also white.

Height: up to 5 inches; cap up to 4 inches in diameter.

Amanita excelsa, common, same habitats, closely resembles the Panther Cap, but has greyish patches on the cap and a fatter stem and appearance.

The Blusher *(Amanita rubescens)*

The Blusher *(Amanita rubescens):*
British Isles, North America.

All types of woodland; also occasionally in fields nearby. Very common. Summer, autumn.

' The cap, convex when young, flattens, mature examples having a slightly striate margin. The torn veil remains as variably sized, soft, mealy patches which may be washed off older examples leaving a smooth, bare cap. The crowded, thin gills are free or adnex; the stem tapers from a bulbous base and is striate above the ring and scaly below, hollowing when mature. The ring is thin, soft and large, spreading downward, and striate on its upper portion. The volva degenerates into small warty scales that may form broken rings around the stem base. The fungus is immediately distinguished from Panther Cap (Panther Amanita) since its flesh reddens when bruised or cut, hence its name. Edible if cooked, but not palatable raw.

Colour: cap dull reddish-brown, tan or dingy flesh, patches greyish; gills white at first become stained or spotted with red as they age; stem white, then with a pink or reddish tint or darker purplish-red areas around base; ring and volva as stem; flesh white but slowly turning pink when cut or as it ages, also pink where slugs or insects make holes; spores white.

Height: up to 9 inches; cap up to 7 inches in diameter.

White-Veiled Amanita *(Amanita calyptroderma):*
North America.

Mixed woodland, or grass-covered areas on edges. Singly or in scattered groups. Common. Autumn.

The smooth cap, convex when young, becomes almost flat on maturity. It is viscid when wet, with a striate margin; the torn veil remaining as one or more large patches. The gills are broad, crowded and free, with a smooth stem which narrows slightly from a large bulbous base. The ring is membranous and spreading downward; the volva thick and cupped. Edible.

Colour: cap variable, creamy-yellow, buff, orange-yellow; gills white or pale yellow; stem white or creamy-yellow; ring yellowish; volva yellowish; flesh white; spores white.

Height: up to 8 inches; cap up to 8 inches in diameter.

The *Amanitopsis* is a genus that resembles the *Amanita* with which it is included by some authorities, but which is described here separately because of the distinguishing feature in that it has no ring on the stem.

Grisette (British Isles), Sheathed Amanitopsis (North America), Sheathed Agaric (North America)
(Amanitopsis vaginata):
British Isles, North America.

Deciduous and coniferous woodlands and on heaths. Singly or in scattered groups. Common. Late summer, autumn.

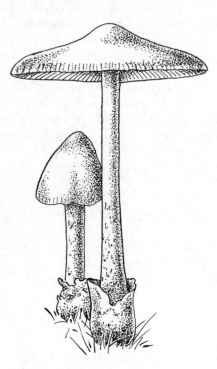

Grisette, Sheathed Amanitopsis, Sheathed Agaric *(Amanitopsis vaginata)*

The cap changes from ovate to bell-shaped, finally flattening with a central boss. It is thin, fragile and smooth with deep radial striations on its margin. Sometimes slightly viscid, it may carry a few patches from the torn veil. The gills are regularly spaced and free; the stem, smooth and slender and tapering from base, becomes hollow and scaly. The volva lies loose and sheath-like around the stem base, deep in the habitat. Edible.

Colour: cap whitish, mouse-grey, pale grey, darker in the central boss; gills white; stem greyish or whitish; volva grey, flesh white; spores white.

Height: up to 6 inches; cap up to 4 inches in diameter.

Strangulated Amanitopsis *(Amanitopsis strangulata):* North America.

Woodlands. Fairly common. Autumn.

The cap, ovate at first becomes flat and then umbonate with deep radial striations on its margin, also having numerous warts. The gills are regularly spaced and free; the stem slender, tapering from the base. The volva usually forms several ridges or collars around the lower stem. Edible.

Colour: cap greyish-brown; gills white; warts dark; stem pale greyish-brown; volva dark; spores white.

Height: up to 5 inches; cap up to 3 inches in diameter.

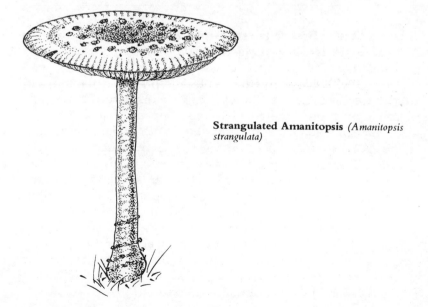

Strangulated Amanitopsis *(Amanitopsis strangulata)*

Tawny Grisette *(Amanitopsis fulva):*
British Isles.
Woodlands and heaths where soil is peaty. Singly or in scattered groups. Common. Summer, autumn.
Similar to Grisette except in colour. It is considered by some mycologists to be a variation. Usually slightly smaller than Grisette, its deep radial striations are clearly defined. Edible. In North America the two colour variations, Grisette and Tawny Grisette, are included under the name Sheathed Amanitopsis.
Colour: cap tawny-brown, reddish-brown, orange-brown; gills whitish; stem whitish or pale tawny; volva yellowish; spores white.

ARMILLARIA

Armillaria is a small genus which has white spores – as do the *Amanitas* – adnate gills, and a membranous ring on the stem, but do not have a volva. Neither does the stem separate easily and cleanly from the cap.

Beech Tuft (British Isles), Slimy Armillaria (North America) *(Armillaria [Oudemansiella] mucida):*
British Isles, North America.
Beech woodlands, on the trunks and branches of dying and dead trees. In clusters, sometimes very numerous on a single tree. Common in suitable habitats. Summer, autumn.
The cap, rounded at first, flattens, with radiating wrinkles and radial striations on its margin; it is translucent and very slimy. The gills are broad, widely spaced and adnate, and may have a decurrent tooth. The thin stem curving away from the upright side of its host trunk, is straighter above the ring, though it may be almost straight and tapering if the habitat – such as top of a horizontal log – allows it. Above the ring it is striate, below it, scaly. The ring is large, wide and striate, spreading downward, and is sited on the upper portion of the stem. The spores are very large and round. It is edible, but unpalatable due to the slimy cap texture.

Plate 5 A cluster of the **Honey Tuft Fungus** or **Honey Agaric** (*Armillaria mellea*), a very destructive fungus, on a beech tree stump.

Plate 6 Several examples of the **Orange Peel Fungus** or **Orange Fairy Cup** (*Peziza [Aleuria] aurantia*) growing in grass. As its name denotes it resembles discarded orange peel.

Plate 7 A group of the **Death Cap** (*Amanita phalloides*). Great care should be exercised when handling this fungus and under no circumstances should it be placed with edible species being gathered to be consumed.

Plate 8 Several examples of the **Triplex Earth Star** (*Geastrum triplex*) which especially occurs in beech woodlands, but in this case they are occurring on oak leaf litter.

Colour: cap glistening white or greyish; gills white; stem white; ring white; spores white.
Height: up to 3 inches; cap up to 6 inches in diameter.

Beech Tuft, Slimy Armillaria *(Armillaria [oudemansiella] mucida)*

Honey Tuft Fungus (British Isles), Honey Armillaria (North America), Honey Mushroom (North America), Honey Agaric (North America), Shoe–String Agaric (North America) *(Armillaria mellea):*
British Isles, North America.

On trunks or at base of living trees and on dead or partly decayed trees and stumps, also on buried wood or above dead roots. In clusters of separate fungi, sometimes very numerous on a tree. Very common. Summer, autumn, early winter.

The cap, convex at first with hairy scales on its edge, may become umbonate, and finally flat with an inrolled, striate margin. Any scales it has will be in the centre. The gills are close and narrow, adnate or slightly decurrent; the stem smooth or fibrillose below the ring and swollen near the base, hollowing with maturity. The ring is large and thick, prominent on the upper stem. Edible, though bitter when raw, the young have a mushroom–like flavour when cooked.

Honey Tuft Fungus
(Armillaria mellea)

This is a very destructive fungus, attacking garden plants, fruit and vegetables and forest trees and causing 'root and butt rot'. It produces long, black strands – rhizomorphs – like leather boot laces (hence one of its North American names) which spread through the soil, sometimes over large distances, attacking trees and other plants. In trees this fungus penetrates under the bark and between the wood, where it flattens and forms a network of white mycelium which can spread upwards and kill the tree. If it is allowed to continue it causes a fibrous white rot in the wood which is often luminous when moist. To protect neighbouring trees, all traces of this fungus and its victim should be removed as soon as possible.
Colour: cap, variable. Young: dull honey yellow, with a greenish tint, when flat pinkish-brown to dark brown, scales brown or blackish; gills white or cream, then pink or spotted, finally brownish with darker spots; stem tan or brown, whitish above the ring, with an olive-yellow or honey-coloured down on stem below ring, hence its other names; ring white with sulphur-yellow edge; flesh white; spores white or cream.

Height: averages 6 inches, depending on site and position; cap up to 6 inches in diameter.

Pine Mushroom *(Armillaria ponderosa):*
North America.
    Coniferous woodlands, especially pine; on soil. Singly or in small groups. Common. Autumn.
    The cap is hemispherical when young, later flattening. Smooth or with fine scales, it is slightly viscid. The narrow gills are crowded and partly attached to the stem, which is solid, slightly viscid; and tapers to the base. The ring is soft and thick. Edible.
Colour: cap white when young then brownish, with brownish scales; gills white, then pinkish or brownish, becoming brown when bruised; stem white; flesh white, creamy-white; spores white.
Height: up to 6 inches; cap up to 8 inches in diameter.

LEPIOTAE

The *Lepiota* genus contains several of the largest fungi as well as a number of small ones. They differ from the *Amanitas* by the absence of the volva, although the stem base may be swollen. Other distinguishing features are the free gills; and a distinct, well-developed ring, which is moveable in species such as The Parasol, although in the smaller species it may be incomplete or absent. Certain species also have an umbo in the centre of a scaly or shaggy cap. The stem and cap separate easily and cleanly.

Crested Lepiota, Stinking Parasol *(Lepiota cristata):*
British Isles, North America.
    Grassy places. Singly or in small groups. Very common. Summer, autumn.
    The cap is conical or bell–shaped, silky, with numerous small scales; the stem slender and smooth while the ring may be small and distinct, or totally absent.
    It may be poisonous, but when crushed it usually has a disagreeable odour, though on occasion it may be mild like a radish aroma.

Colour: cap white, cap scales rusty red-brown; gills white; stem pale pink-brown; spores white.
Height: up to 2 inches; cap up to 2 inches in diameter.

Crested Lepiota, Stinking Parasol
(Lepiota cristata)

Lepiota acutesquamosa:
British Isles.

In gardens, woodlands and similar, wherever leaf mould is present. Fairly common. Summer, autumn.

It is normally identified by the numerous pointed warts on the conical cap, though these may be absent from older specimens. There are many gills, which may be forked; the stem is thick, and scaly below the ring, but there is no distinct swollen base. The immovable ring has warts on its underside. The fungus is harmless, but inedible because the flesh has a bitter flavour.

Colour: cap reddish-brown; warts tawny or reddish-brown; gills white; stem whitish above the ring, brown below; ring whitish above, underside warts brown; flesh and spores white.
Height: up to 4 inches; cap up to 4 inches in diameter.

Morgan's Lepiota, Green-Gilled Lepiota *(Lepiota morganii [molybdites])*:

North America.

Found in similar habitats to the Parasol which it closely resembles. Fairly common. Summer, autumn.

The cap is rounded, like a drumstick when young, becoming the typical parasol shape with shaggy scales. The gills are close and free and the stem thick, swollen at the base. The ring is also thick. Poisonous.

Colour: cap whitish; scales whitish; gills pale green; stem whitish; ring white; spores dull green.

Height: up to 8 inches; cap up to 8 inches in diameter.

Parasol Mushroom *(Lepiota procera):*
British Isles, North America.

Clearings in woodlands, among grass at the edge of a copse and similar habitats. Fairly common. Autumn.

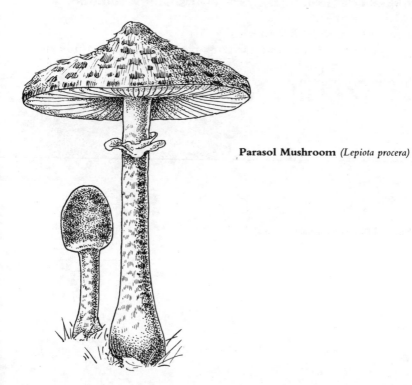

Parasol Mushroom *(Lepiota procera)*

The young cap is almost spherical; with its stem, shaped like a drumstick, expanding later to the typical parasol shape with a definite umbo. The cap has numerous shaggy scales which also form a fringe around the margin. The gills are free; the stem tapers from its swollen base and separates easily from the cap, leaving a socket created by a ridge of tissue. The young stem has a felt-like surface, but this eventually cracks into irregular scales. There is a large, thick, movable double ring. Edible, and considered by connoisseurs to be excellent.

Colour: cap greyish-brown; shaggy scales dull brown; gills white; stem, young brown, later irregular scales brown, whitish above ring; ring white above, brown below; flesh white; spores white.

Height: up to 11 inches; cap up to 8 inches in diameter. One of the largest fungi in the British Isles.

Ragged Parasol, Shaggy Parasol, Shaggy Lepiota
(Lepiota rhacodes):
British Isles, North America.

Open woodlands and gardens, particularly on humus rich soil and compost heaps. Singly or in groups. Common. Summer, autumn.

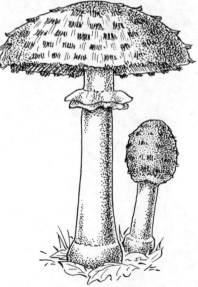

Ragged Parasol *(Lepiota rhacodes)*

86

The young cap is almost spherical, its later stages similar to the Parasol but being more rounded with a weak or absent umbo. In North America it closely resembles Morgan's Lepiota. The flat scales, larger than those of Parasol, are in concentric rings and more shaggy with ends which sometimes turn up. The gills are free, broad and close; the smooth stem may be shorter and thicker than in Parasol, tapering from a bulbous base. Near the top of the stem is a thick movable ring with a fringe like a cap margin. Edible. Colour: cap paler than Parasol, fawn, may be white with a darker centre; gills white; stem white, the snake–like irregular markings of Parasol are absent; ring white; flesh of cap and stem white, becoming reddish if cut or bruised; spores white. Height: up to 9 inches; cap up to 7 inches in diameter.

Smooth Lepiota, White Lepiota (*Lepiota naucina [naucinoides]*):
North America.

Open grassy areas. Singly or colonial. Common. Summer, autumn.

The cap is ovoid when young, then convex or almost flat. It is smooth, but occasionally irregularly cracked. The gills are free, broad and close; the stem, smooth and solid, tapering from a bulbous base. Hollowing in maturity, it separates easily from the cap. The membranous ring is usually movable. It is considered edible and quite choice by some authorities while others believe it mildly poisonous. The truth could be that it is poison only to certain persons, causing nausea and vomiting. It resembles the very toxic Spring Amanita or Fools' Mushroom.
Colour: cap white; gills white, then pinkish, finally pale reddish-brown, changing to smoky-brown; stem, ring, flesh and spores white.
Height: up to 6 inches; cap up to 4 inches in diameter.

Yellow Lepiota (*Lepiota lutea*):
North America.

In greenhouses or in soil of pot plants kept in damp

conditions. Singly or in groups. Fairly common. Summer, autumn.

The cap ovoid matures to bell-shaped and finally rounded like Shaggy Parasol; cap and stem have fluffy scales while the stem is narrow, tapering from a slightly bulbous base. There is a prominent ring towards the top of the stem. Probably poisonous.

Colour: cap sulphur-yellow; gills pale yellow; stem and ring sulphur-yellow; spores white.

Height: up to 3 inches; cap up to 1½ inches in diameter.

Yellow Lepiota *(Lepiota lutea)*

TRICHOLOMATACEAE

The genus *Tricholoma* does not have a distinct ring or volva; the gills are always notched or curved upward near the point of attachment to the stem, and the stem itself is fibrous, the flesh being continuous with that of the cap. The spores are white in the majority of the species, otherwise flesh pink. While some of the *Tricholoma* are edible, others are inedible but harmless, and none of the British species is poisonous although the

North American Leopard Tricholoma can prove fatal if eaten. Those species with pinkish spores have recently been separated from the *Tricholoma* and placed in their own genus *Lepista* or *Rhodopaxillus*, but are retained here for the sake of convenience and to avoid confusion.

Blewit (British Isles, North America), Blue Leg (British Isles), Masked Tricholoma (North America) *(Tricholoma personatum [Lepista saeva]):*
British Isles, North America.

Among grass in pastures and meadows, also on downland. Singly, in groups, or forming large fairy rings. Common. Late autumn, early winter.

Blewit, Blue Leg, Masked Tricholoma
(Tricholoma personatum [Lepista saeva])

The cap is smooth and hemispherical, with an incurved margin when young, becoming convex and finally flat or with its margin irregularly upcurved. The broad, rounded gills are crowded and sinuate, sometimes free of the stem, which is short, stout and solid, with scaly fibrils but becoming smooth when mature. The flesh is thick and soft, spongy when wet, and identified immediately by its colour. Edible, with a pleasant aroma and flavour, and formerly a culinary rival to the Common Field and Horse Mushrooms, it was once

89

gathered for sale in Covent Garden and markets in the Midlands, and may still occasionally be found being sold in some areas in Britain.

Colour: cap, variable, violet–grey, pale grey, or brownish tinged with lilac or purple, fading to pale tan, buff, occasionally dirty white; gills bluish or whitish when young becoming lavender, greyish-buff or pinkish; stem bluish or lavender fading to whitish, scaly fibrils lilac or dark violet; flesh whitish when dry, greyish or lavender when wet; spores flesh or pale pink.

Height: up to 3 inches; cap up to 5 inches in diameter.

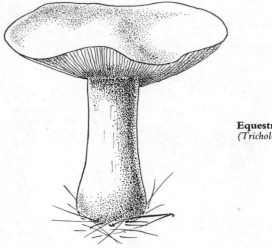

Equestrian Tricholoma
(Tricholoma equestre [flavovirens])

Equestrian Tricholoma (North America) *(Tricholoma equestre [flavovirens])*:

British Isles, North America.

Pine plantations; particularly on sandy soil. Fairly common. Summer, autumn.

The cap, rounded and flattened, may have an irregular waved margin. Viscid when wet, it is similar to Sulphurous Tricholoma, but is of different colour; the cap fibrillose; the stem thick. Edible, with no unpleasant aroma.

Colour: cap greenish-yellow, with scales giving it a reddish-

brown tint in centre; gills sulphur–yellow; stem greenish-yellow; spores white.
Height: up to 3 inches; cap up to 4 inches in diameter.

Grey Tricholoma (North America) *(Tricholoma terreum):*
British Isles, North America.

Coniferous and deciduous woodlands. Singly, in clusters, sometimes in large numbers. Common, sometimes very common. Late autumn.

The cap is rounded and umbonate, with a covering of fine, silky fibrils or scales; the stem is mealy at its summit. Edible, with no aroma.
Colour: cap dark grey; scales dark; gills grey; stem greyish-white; flesh white; spores white.
Height: up to 3 inches; cap up to 3 inches in diameter.

Grey Tricholoma *(Tricholoma terreum)*

Leopard Tricholoma *(Tricholoma pardinum):*
North America.

Under conifers. Fairly common. Autumn.

The cap is rounded, with numerous scales; the stem thick. Poisonous. May be fatal if consumed. Could be confused with Edible Mushroom, but remember its different habitat.

Leopard Tricholoma *(Tricholoma pardinum)*

Colour: cap white, scales dark grey; stem, flesh and spores white.
Height: up to 5 inches; cap up to 6 inches in diameter.

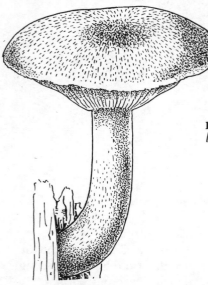

Red-Haired Tricholoma *(Tricholoma [Tricholomopsis] rutilans)*

Red-Haired Tricholoma (North America) *(Tricholoma [Tricholomopsis] rutilans):*
British Isles, North America.

Pine woodlands, on or close to pine stumps. Fairly common. Autumn.

The cap is a rough bell-shape when young; finally flattening, with a small umbo. There is a thick covering of small downy scales, particularly in young specimens. The gills are broad, thick, crowded and sinuate; the stem thick and scaly. Harmless, but not edible. No aroma.
Colour: cap, ground yellow, covering scales dark red or reddish-purple; gills yellow; stem pale yellow, scales purple; flesh pale yellow; spores white.
Height: up to 4 inches; cap up to 6 inches in diameter.

Soap-Scented Tricholoma (British Isles), Soapy Tricholoma (North America) *(Tricholoma saponaceum):*
British Isles, North America.

All types of woodland. Singly or in small groups. Common. Late summer, autumn.

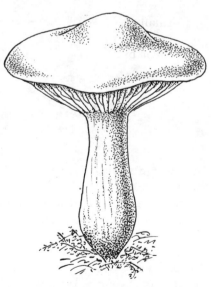

Soap-Scented Tricholoma, Soapy Tricholoma
(Tricholoma saponaceum)

The cap is rounded, but may have an irregular marginal outline; the thick stem may taper from the base. The cap is

93

never viscid, but is scaly in dry weather. Identified by its flavour and an aroma of kitchen soap. Harmless but not palatable.

Colour: cap grey or dingy brown, may have an olive-green tinge, stem buff; as fungus ages has flesh pink areas on the stem and finally on cap; gills buff; with blue–grey margins, sometimes red spots; flesh and gills become pink or red if broken or bruised; spores white.

Height: up to 4 inches; cap up to 4 inches in diameter.

St George's Mushroom
(Tricholoma gambosum)

St George's Mushroom *(Tricholoma gambosum):*
British Isles.

On open grass in meadows and pastures or grassy areas near hedges where hawthorn and wild damson (sloe) grow; also in undergrowth on margin of woodlands. Forms fairy rings on hillside and downland turf; prefers limestone and chalk soils. Not common. April, May, June.

The cap is rounded and wide, but may be flattened, usually having an irregular, waved margin which may also be turned inwards. It is smooth with the texture of a kid glove. The gills

94

are broad, close and crowded, sinuate or adnexed with a slight decurrent tooth and the stem is thick, stout and short. It may be curved or irregular, and, slightly swollen at the base. An edible and an excellent early species, with a pleasant flavour and a mealy aroma when cut, but it must not be confused with the poisonous *Inocybe patouillardii,* also occurring at the same time, which is similar but with dark brown spores and no aroma. So-called because it may appear about St George's Day, April 23rd, but is more plentiful in May.

Colour: cap pale creamy-white to yellowish, pale tan, light buff or pinkish-buff with age; gills whitish or pale cream; stem, as cap, whitish or light buff; flesh and spores white.
Height: up to 3 inches; cap up to 3 inches in diameter.

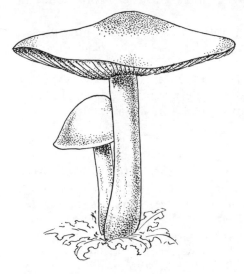

Sulphurous Tricholoma
(Tricholoma sulphureum)

Sulphurous Tricholoma *(Tricholoma sulphureum):*
British Isles.

Mixed broadleafed woodlands, particularly where oak is plentiful. Common. Summer, autumn.

The rounded, flattened cap is usually irregularly shaped, with a split margin. The gills are thick and distant, emarginate; the stem curved and twisted, fibrous at first but finally hollow. Recognized by its colour and unpleasant

aroma like coal–gas. Harmless, but not palatable due to its smell.
Colour: cap, gills and stem lemon–yellow or sulphur–yellow; flesh yellow; spores white.
Height: up to 3 inches; cap up to 3 inches in diameter.

Tricholoma argyraceum – Tricholoma scalpturatum:
British Isles.
   Broadleafed woodlands. Common. Summer.
Similar to *Tricholoma terreum*, but has white gills, also a mealy aroma.

Tricholoma columbetta:
British Isles.
   Leafy woodlands; on acid, sandy soil. Fairly common. Late summer, autumn.
   The cap is flattened, smooth and silky, sometimes glossy; the stem may be more slender, narrower near the base. Edible.
Colour: cap white, may have a few bluish or pinkish spots or areas; gills white; stem white; flesh white; spores white.
Height: up to 3 inches; cap up to 4 inches in diameter.

Tricholoma fulvum:
British Isles.
   On peaty and damp soil beneath broad-leaved trees, especially in open birch woodlands. Common. Autumn.
   The cap is rounded, with an umbo, slimy or viscid when wet; the stem pointed at the base, becoming hollow. Harmless, but has an unpleasant, rancid, mealy aroma.
Colour: cap bright reddish–brown; stem similar but paler at the summit; gills pale yellow but brown–spotted with age; flesh, cap white, stem yellow; spores white.
Height: up to 3 inches; cap up to 3 inches in diameter.

Tricholoma portentosum:
British Isles.
   Coniferous woodlands, particularly under pine trees. Fairly common. Autumn.
   The cap is typical, fibrillose towards the centre; the stem thick and stout. Edible with no aroma.

Colour: cap greyish-brown, fibrils dark, giving cap a very dark, near-black centre; gills yellowish; stem whitish with a yellow tint; spores white.
Height: up to 4 inches; cap up to 5 inches in diameter.

Tricholoma psammopus:
British Isles.

Occurs only in open larch woodlands or around larch trees. Uncommon. Summer.

Similar to *Tricholoma fulvum*, but smaller, the slender stem having a brownish, granular, scaly surface, the flesh also being pale brown rather than yellow.

Tricholoma ustale:
British Isles.

Broad-leaved woodlands on boggy areas. Fairly common. Autumn.

Similar to *Tricholoma fulvum* but the cap wider and the cap margin irregular and wavy and the meal-like aroma absent. The gills whitish when young, becoming brown-spotted with age.

Wood Blewits (British Isles, North America), Blue Cap (British Isles), Naked Tricholoma (North America)
(Tricholoma nudum [Lepista nuda]):
British Isles, North America.

Woodlands and gardens; on fallen leaves, on compost heaps. Singly or in clusters. Very common. Late autumn, continually while climate suitable until winter frosts.

The cap is convex when young, becoming almost flattened and may be depressed in the centre; smooth, with a wavy incurved margin. The gills are narrow, crowded, sinuate or slightly decurrent. The stem, taller and more slender than Blewit, is solid and fibrillose with a mealy texture; its base may have violet, cottony mycelial strands. Edible, with a pleasant fruity aroma. Relished and formerly much sought by connoisseurs who considered it equal to the Blewit.
Colour: cap lilac with a purplish hue, reddish-brown or

97

brownish-violet as it ages; gills lilac or bluish-violet, but reddish as they age; stem as cap or paler; flesh whitish when dry, bluish-lilac when wet; spores flesh-coloured or pinkish. Height: up to 4 inches; cap up to 4 inches in diameter.

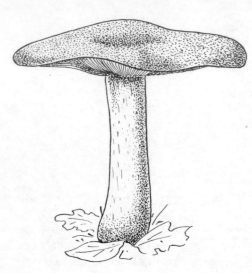

Wood Blewits
(Tricholoma nudum
[Lepista nuda])

CLITOCYBEAE

The genus *Clitocybe* is similar to the *Tricholoma*, with white spores and a fleshy, fibrillose stem which is inseparable from the cap, but *Clitocybe* has decurrent gills and caps shaped like spinning tops or funnels. There is no ring on the stem.

Clitocybe dealbata:
British Isles.

Grassy habitats, also in mushroom beds where it can be a dangerous nuisance. In groups. Fairly common. Late summer, autumn.

Similar to its close relation *Clitocybe rivulosa* in height and shape, but its finely powdered cap is pure white, sometimes with a faint brown or yellow tint, but not zoned. Poisonous. Has a mealy aroma.

False Champignon *(Clitocybe rivulosa):*
British Isles.

Grassy habitats, preferring short turf. Sometimes appears among edible Fairy Ring Champignon and known as the False Champignon for this reason. In groups. Common. Late summer, autumn.

The flattened or umbilicate cap is wrinkled, with a fine powdery bloom when young; the margin incurved. The gills are crowded and decurrent, and the stem may be twisted or mis-shapen. Poisonous. Only a slight aroma.

Colour: cap whitish when young with alternating darker and paler zones, becoming pale greyish-flesh or pale yellowish with a whitish margin; gills paler than cap; stem, same as cap; flesh white; spores white.

Height: up to 2 inches, cap up to 2 inches in diameter, but usually exceeding the height.

False Champignon *(Clitocybe rivulosa)*

Clitocybe vibecina:
British Isles.

Pine woodlands; among bracken. Often very numerous and forming rings. Very common. Autumn.

The smooth cap is depressed in the centre becoming funnel-shaped, with a striate margin; the stem may be curved. The

99

gills are narrow, crowded and decurrent. May be harmless, but not edible. Has a mealy aroma.

Colour: cap and flesh both greyish when wet, whitish when dry; gills whitish or pale grey; stem grey with woolly white at the base, white at the summit; spores white.

Height: up to 2½ inches; cap up to 2 inches in diameter.

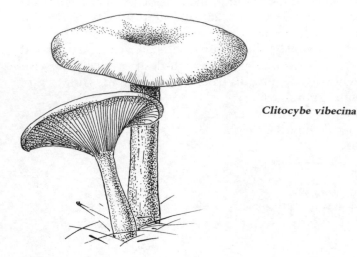

Clitocybe vibecina

Clouded Clitocybe *(Clitocybe nebularis):*
British Isles, North America.

Deciduous woodlands. In large groups or rings. Common. Late autumn.

The cap is convex, fleshy and smooth, with a powdery bloom when young; it may become depressed later. The gills are thin and narrow, very crowded, adnate then decurrent; the solid stem is fibrillose, slightly thicker close to the base, spongy at first, then hollow. Edible but indigestible, with a disagreeable aroma.

Colour: cap pale grey, with a darker centre; gills whitish or pale grey; stem whitish or pale grey as cap; flesh white; spores creamy-white.

Height: up to 5 inches; cap up to 7 inches in diameter.

100

Clouded Clitocybe *(Clitocybe nebularis)*

Club-Footed Clitocybe *(Clitocybe clavipes):*
British Isles.

Coniferous and deciduous woodlands, particularly under beech trees. Very common. Late autumn, early winter.

Club-Footed Clitocybe
(Clitocybe clavipes)

Similar to Clouded Clitocybe, but smaller, with the cap top-shaped, umbonate when young, later having a shallow depression. The gills are distant, thin, broad and very decurrent, the stem fibrillose, with a distinct swelling towards the spongy base. Harmless but not edible.

Colour: cap olive-brown or greyish-brown, paler on margin, darker in centre; gills cream or primrose-yellowish; stem as cap but paler; flesh greyish; spores white.

Height: up to 2 inches; cap up to 3 inches in diameter.

Common Funnel Cap *(Clitocybe infundibuliformis)*

Common Funnel Cap *(Clitocybe infundibuliformis):*
British Isles.

Woodlands, heaths, commons; among debris and grass. In groups. Very common. Mid–summer, autumn.

The funnel-shaped cap has a margin which may be irregular, wavy, upturned; the gills are crowded and very decurrent; the stem hairy and slightly swollen at its base. Harmless, but not edible, with an aroma of bitter almonds.

Colour: cap, variable, pinkish-tan, yellowish–buff, rusty-brown; gills white; stem paler than cap; flesh and spores white.

Height: up to 3 inches; cap up to $2\frac{1}{2}$ inches in diameter.

Deceiving Clitocybe, Jack-o'-Lantern *(Clitocybe illudens):*
North America.

In woodlands; on logs, tree stumps. In close groups. Common. Autumn.

The cap is flattened, with a central depression; the margin may be irregular. The gills are crowded and decurrent, and the slender stems may be twisted in a crowded cluster. Poisonous and luminous.

Colour: cap, stem, rusty-brown, with paler areas; gills brown; spores white.

Height: up to 7 inches; cap up to 5 inches in diameter.

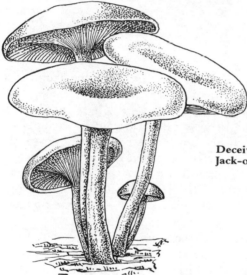

**Deceiving Clitocybe,
Jack-o'-Lantern** *(Clitocybe illudens)*

**Fragrant Clitocybe (British Isles, North America),
Sweet-Scented Clitocybe (North America), Anise-
Scented Clitocybe (North America), Anise Cap (British
Isles)** *(Clitocybe odora):*
British Isles, North America.

Shady coniferous and mixed woodland; among dead leaves and debris. Scattered singly, or in small groups. Common. Late summer, autumn.

103

Fragrant Clitocybe (*Clitocybe odora*)

The young cap is convex, flattening, then irregularly upturned and lobed; smooth, with a downy, wavy and incurved margin. The gills are thin, crowded and slightly decurrent; the stem slightly swollen close to its base, solid becoming hollow. Edible, with a strong but pleasantly fragrant aroma and flavour of anise even after being dried, which makes it useful for flavouring. Not to be confused with the small and pale brown *Clitocybe suaveolens* of coniferous woodlands, or the pale yellowish-brown *Clitocybe fragrans*, both of which also have a similar anise aroma.

Colour: cap sea blue-green or glaucous greyish-green, fades as it ages, appears more blue in wet weather; gills paler than cap, glaucous; stem greenish or whitish-green, paler than cap; flesh white or pale green; spores white.

Height: up to 2½ inches; cap up to 3 inches in diameter.

Giant Clitocybe (*Clitocybe gigantea*):
British Isles, North America.

Coniferous woodlands; open grassy areas. Singly or in groups. Common. Late summer, autumn.

When young, the cap is rounded with an incurved margin, then flattening with a central depression and finally broad funnel-shaped; smooth and fleshy. The gills are crowded, narrow, may be forked, and are joined by veins near the stem; the stem is fibrillose, glabrous, short and thick, either tapering downwards or cylindrical. The base may be swollen. Edible. Has a pleasant, if weak aroma, but is not relished as it is tough when prepared.

Colour: cap ivory-white, cream to buff, with a central tint of tan when young, entirely tan as it ages; gills whitish to pale tan, darkening with age; stem tan on summit, whitish on lower portion; flesh and spores white.

Height: up to 4 inches; cap up to 12 inches in diameter, but huge examples have occurred.

Orange Clitocybe (North America), Yellow Clitocybe (North America), False Chanterelle (British Isles, North America) *(Clitocybe [Hygrophoropsis] aurantiaca):*

British Isles, North America.

Shady coniferous and mixed woodlands, on heaths; on humus or decayed wood. Singly or in groups. Very common. Late summer, autumn.

Orange Clitocybe, Yellow Clitocybe, False Chanterelle
(Clitocybe [Hygrophoropsis] aurantiaca)

The cap is flat when young with an incurved margin, later slightly depressed in the centre or funnel-shaped, with the margin wavy and incurved, curling upward or downward. The gills are thin, narrow, crowded, frequently forked and deeply decurrent; the stem, slender and elastic, sometimes

105

curved, is smooth or finely tomentose. Usually solid, sometimes hollow. Though it resembles Chanterelle, it has true gills and not folds, and lacks the apricot aroma and pinkish-buff spores of Chanterelle. Formerly considered poisonous, it is now known to be harmless, but its flavour is unpleasant.

Colour: cap, variable, pale yellow-buff to bright orange, darker or brownish in centre; gills deep orange or orange-red; stem yellowish, orange or reddish-brown; flesh yellowish to pale orange; spores white.

Height: up to 4 inches; cap up to 3 inches in diameter.

Tawny Funnel Cap *(Clitocybe flaccida):*
British Isles.

Coniferous and broadleafed woodlands. In large groups or fairy rings. Common. Late autumn, early winter.

Tawny Funnel Cap
(Clitocybe flaccida)

The cap is clearly funnel-shaped, with a wavy or lobed downward curving margin. The gills are narrow and crowded, deeply decurrent, curving to the shape of the cap; the smooth stem curves to a slightly wider white-woolly base; elastic. Harmless, but with a sour aroma and bitter flavour, it is not considered edible.

Colour: cap reddish-brown or tan; gills white to yellowish

106

then reddish as they age; stem pale brownish; flesh white when young becoming pale tan and rusty-brown; spores white. Height: up to 3 inches; cap up to 4 inches in diameter.

LACCARIA

The genus *Laccaria* differs chiefly from *Clitocybe* in having large warty or spiny globular white spores that give the mature, thick, broad, separated gills a visibly powdery appearance. The gills are also adnate, decurrent or with a decurrent tooth.

**Amethyst Laccaria,
Amethyst Deceiver**
(Laccaria amethystina)

**Amethyst Laccaria (British Isles, North America),
Amethyst Deceiver (British Isles)** *(Laccaria amethystina):*
British Isles, North America.

Shady, damp woodlands. In groups. Common. Summer, autumn.

Similar in shape and size to its close relative Waxy Laccaria, it is considered by some mycologists to be a variety of it; the two sometimes occur together in the same habitat. Edible, but of poor quality with little flesh.

Colour: the entire fungus is amethyst or deep violet, occasionally brownish, the violet or amethyst being more pronounced when moist; when dry becomes a paler purplish-grey; gill colour fades less rapidly than Waxy Laccaria.

Height: up to 4 inches; cap up to 2 inches in diameter.

Waxy Laccaria (North America), Waxy Deceiver (British Isles) *(Laccaria laccata):*
British Isles, North America.

Open woodlands, open fields, heaths, peat bogs and moist places. In groups. Very common. Late summer, autumn, early winter.

Waxy Laccaria, Waxy Deceiver
(Laccaria laccata)

The cap is variable in appearance, basically changing from convex to flat with maturity, the centre being either raised or depressed, either slightly scaly or smooth. Similarly, the wavy margin curves either up or down and the stem may be curved or twisted. The gills are thick, broad and distant, adnate with a decurrent tooth; the stem fibrous, hollowing with maturity, having woolly white mycelium at its base. Edible, but poor quality, with little flesh.

Colour: cap, variable, pale flesh-red, rose-red, reddish-brown, brick-red or lilac-rose when wet, becoming ruddy-flesh, greyish, buff, dull orange or yellowish when dry; gills flesh–pink when young becoming reddish; stem similar to cap except at base; flesh pinkish or reddish; spores colourless. Height: up to 4 inches; cap up to 2 inches in diameter.

COLLYBIEAE

The *Collybieae* is a very large group of fungi from which only a few examples can be quoted in a book of this length. Specimens have tough, cartilaginous stems which are inseparable from the cap. The gills are either adnate, decurrent or free, and the spores white. The group is subdivided into the *Collybia, Asterophora, Marasmius, Mycena* and *Omphalia*.

COLLYBIA

The genus *Collybia* has tough, smooth, cartilaginous stems, but no ring or volva. The smooth membranous caps have an inrolled margin when young, the gills being adnate, adnexed or free. The spores are smooth and small, either white or pale pink.

Broad-Gilled Collybia, Broad-Gilled Agaric *(Collybia [Tricholomopsis] platyphylla)*

Broad-Gilled Collybia (North America), Broad-Gilled Agaric (British Isles) *(Collybia [Tricholomopsis] platyphylla):*
British Isles, North America.

Broadleafed woodlands; on or connected to tree stumps or decayed wood. Fairly common. Midsummer, autumn.

The cap is wide with thin, dark fibrils forming radial streaks; the margin may be upcurved. The gills are very broad and distantly spaced, the gill edges having large, thin-walled cystidia; the stem is stout, more fibrous than cartilaginous, with strong, rootlike, branching strands of white mycelium at the base that may extend several feet through the habitat. They are pulled up when the stem is picked, thus identifying the species immediately. Harmless, but inedible.
Colour: cap grey, smoky-brown, blackish-brown; gills white; stem pale grey; flesh and spores white.
Height: up to 5 inches; cap up to 6 inches in diameter.

Bunched Collybia, Tufted Collybia *(Collybia acervata):*
North America.

On rotten logs or on a thick humus layer in woodlands and elsewhere. In dense clusters. Common. Late summer, autumn.

The cap is bell-shaped when young, becoming rounded; the gills narrow, close, and almost free; the stem slender and long, several may be joined in the habitat for part of their length. Edible, but usually unpalatable, with a bitter flavour.
Colour: cap dull pale brown or purplish-brown, whitish when dry; gills pale brown; stem reddish-brown; spores whitish.
Height: up to 3 inches; cap up to 2 inches in diameter.

Buttery Collybia (North America), Greasy Tough Shank (British Isles), Greasy Club Foot (British Isles) *(Collybia butyracea):*
British Isles, North America.

Woodlands. Very common. Late summer, autumn, early winter.

The bell-shaped cap has a distinct central umbo and is smooth, greasy or buttery to touch when wet. The gills are thin, broad, crowded, and almost free; the stem cartilaginous and tapered, with a thickened spongy base (see *Clitocybe*

110

clavipes). Edible, but not palatable, being tough.

Colour: cap brown, drying paler on margin to umbo, always a darker brown umbo; gills whitish or greyish-brown; stem as cap; spores white or pale pinkish.

Height: up to 4 inches; cap up to 3 inches in diameter.

Buttery Collybia, Greasy Tough Shank, Greasy Club Foot
(Collybia butyracea)

Collybia tuberosa:

British Isles.

On old decaying fungi on the earth. In groups. Common. Summer, autumn.

The cap is flat, the gills narrow and crowded, and the stem thin, long and hairy near the base. This fungus develops from a small, red-brown, egg-shaped sclerotium buried in the habitat.

Colour: cap opaque white, with yellow tints near centre; gills white; stem mealy white; spores white.

Height: up to 2 inches; cap up to $\frac{3}{4}$ inch in diameter.

COLLYBIA CIRRHATA is similar to *C. tuberosa* in shape and habitat but is usually smaller. The cap may be centrally depressed and the stem very slender, with a fibrillose twisted rooting area. It develops from a small, yellow, oval sclerotium buried among decaying leaves or humus where a fungus has rotted.

Collybia tuberosa

Rooting Collybia (North America), Rooting Shank (British Isles) *(Collybia [Oudemansiella] radicata):*
British Isles, North America.

Open woodlands; on earth containing decaying wood. Singly or several in a group. Common. Early summer, late autumn.

Rooting Collybia, Rooting Shank
(Collybia [Oudemansiella] radicata)

The cap is convex when young, then flat, with a small central umbo which may be surrounded by radial furrows; it is slimy when wet. The gills are broad, quite thick, distant, adnexed or adnate with a decurrent tooth; the stem tough, tall and slender, furrowed and twisted, hollow, with a long, tapered root-like extension penetrating the habitat and attached by strands to the organic matter in the soil. Edible, but not usually palatable, being tough.
Colour: cap yellowish-brown or greyish-brown; gills white; stem pale brown; flesh and spores white.
Height: up to 8 inches from habitat surface; cap up to 4 inches in diameter.

Russet Shank *(Collybia [Marasmius] dryophila)*:
British Isles.
Open woodlands, especially under oak trees. In groups. Common. Late spring, summer, early autumn.
Resembles Fairy Ring Champignon, but has a different habitat. The gills are narrow and crowded; the stem tough, flexible and slender.
Colour: variable, cap pale to dark yellowish-brown; gills white or have pale yellow tints; stem brown, reddish-brown at base; spores white.
Height: up to 4 inches; cap up to 2 inches in diameter.

Spindle Shank (British Isles), Spindly Foot (British Isles) *(Collybia fusipes)*:
British Isles.
Found at the base of trees, particularly beech and oak. In large groups. Common. Late spring, summer, autumn, early winter.
The cap is rounded when young, becoming flat; smooth, with a central umbo though the margin may be inrolled and split in several places. The gills are broad, thick and distant, adnexed or adnate but eventually separating from the stem; the stem is tough, furrowed and twisted, tapering to the thin base. This fungus grows year after year from a dark-coloured underground mass of fungal tissue attached to the roots of the living tree and which may remain there for numerous years. Harmless, with a spicy aroma, but of little value as food.

113

Colour: cap dark reddish-brown or liver when wet, paler when dry; gills white then paler than cap colour, spotted with red-brown as they age; stem as cap, but darker at base; flesh pale reddish-brown; spores white.

Height: up to 6 inches; cap up to 4 inches in diameter.

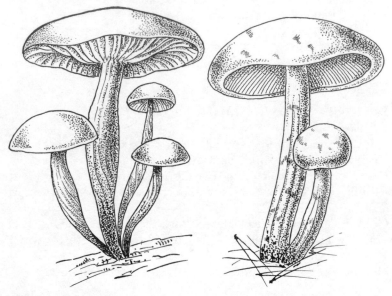

Spindle Shank, Spindly Foot
(Collybia fusipes)

Spotted Tough Shank *(Collybia maculata)*

Spotted Tough Shank *(Collybia maculata):*
British Isles.

Mixed and coniferous woodland; among bracken and similar undergrowth. In groups. Very common. Midsummer, autumn.

The cap is convex and smooth, with an incurved margin when young; the gills are very narrow and densely crowded, their edges perhaps toothed. The stem is firm, tough and furrowed, sometimes wavy, and tall, tapering upwards from the thickened lower portion below which it tapers to a blunt point at the root-like base. Harmless.

Colour: cap, gills and stem white when young, later with brownish–red blotches; flesh white; spores white or very pale pinkish.
Height: up to 5 inches; cap up to 5 inches in diameter.

Velvet Shank (British Isles), Velvet Foot (British Isles), Velvet-Footed Collybia (North America), Velvet–Stem Collybia (North America), Velvet–Stemmed Agaric (British Isles), Winter Fungus (British Isles) *(Collybia [Flammulina] velutipes):*
British Isles, North America.

On living or dead trunks, branches, stumps or logs, old gorse bushes and other shrubs. In clusters. Fairly common. Late autumn, early winter, surviving mild winters into spring.

The cap is convex when young, later flattening; smooth, it becomes viscous when wet. The margin, sometimes finely striate, may be upcurved with age. The gills are broad, distant, adnexed; the tough stem, usually curving upward from the base, is covered with dense velvet and may be solid or hollow. Edible; eaten in North America where it is prized because other edible fungi are then absent, though its flavour is weak and watery.

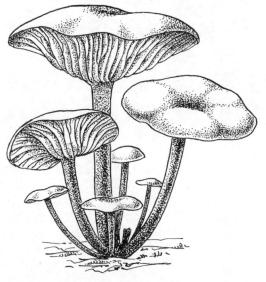

Velvet Shank *(Collybia [Flammulina] velutipes)*

Colour: cap bright yellow with darker yellowish–brown centre and sometimes an orange tint; margin paler; gills yellowish becoming darker as they age; stem yellowish when young, later reddish–brown on upper portion, darker brown on lower portion; flesh yellowish; spores white.

Height: up to 2½ inches; cap up to 3 inches in diameter.

ASTEROPHORA – NYCTALIS

The genus *Asterophora* or *Nyctalis* is also known as the Pick–A–Back Toadstool because it occurs as a parasite of Agaric fungi, particularly the *Russula*. Specimens are small, with weak, fold–like gills, a characteristic which induces certain mycologists to place them with the *Cantharellaceae*, though their habitat gives a clue to their identity.

Asterophora lycoperdiodes [Nyctalis asterophora]

Asterophora lycoperdiodes [Nyctalis asterophora]: British Isles.

On decaying examples of *Russula nigricans* and *Russula adusta*. In clusters. Common, more so in wet weather. Early autumn.

The cap is conical, true gills infrequently occurring, being hidden by a powdery, mealy mass of chlamydospores quickly developing on the cap; the stem is short, and may be curved or twisted. Not edible. Has a rancid aroma.

Colour: cap white at first, then brownish or fawn with the chlamydospores; stem white, then brownish.

Height: up to 1 inch; cap up to ½ inch in diameter.

116

Asterophora parasitica [Nyctalis parasitica]:
British Isles.

On decaying Agarics, especially *Russula*. In clusters. Fairly common. Early autumn.

Similar to *Asterophora lycoperdiodes* (*Nyctalis asterophora*) but chlamydospores develop on the thick gills, so the smooth cap retains its conical shape. Has a foul, noxious aroma.
Colour: cap grey; gills covered by brownish chlamydospores; thin stem grey.
Height: up to 1 inch; cap up to ½ inch in diameter.

MARASMIUS

The *Marasmius* genus has some characteristics similar to *Collybia*, but generally with a smaller, tougher, leathery sporophore, shrivelling when dry without suffering harm and reviving when moistened to shed spores. The genus contains the familiar Fairy Ring Champignon relished when cooked or dried as a flavouring. The other members of the Marasmius genus are harmless, but many are too small, with wiry, tough stems, to be worth eating.

Black-Stemmed Marasmius, Horse-Hair Toadstool *(Marasmius androsaceus)*

Black-Stemmed Marasmius (North America), Horse-Hair Toadstool (British Isles) *(Marasmius androsaceus):*
British Isles, North America.

Woodlands, especially coniferous; on the fallen pine and spruce needles and twigs where it may be present in a carpet of hundreds. Also occurs among or on heather, if the habitat is

117

very moist. The fungi are produced from a loose mass of horse-hair-like black mycelium, the strands of which wind around, penetrate and kill the heather branches. Common. Summer, autumn.

The finely wrinkled cap is flat, with a central depression, and striate; the gills are thin, few, and widely spaced; the stem long, thin, rigid and wiry, curved or wavy.

Colour: cap pale reddish–brown, central depression darker or clay-brown, finally black; gills white or pinkish; stem shiny, brownish–black; spores white.

Height: up to $2\frac{1}{2}$ inches; cap up to $\frac{1}{2}$ inch in diameter.

Fairy Ring Champignon (British Isles), Fairy Ring Marasmius (North America) *(Marasmius oreades)*:
British Isles, North America.

In grassland, downland, lawns, golf courses, etc., especially after rain. May be in a group of a few, a partial ring, a loose circle, or a fairy ring of hundreds. Its presence creates the unsightly and often unwelcome bare circle of dead grass with a dark green grass border in the short turf. Common. Summer, autumn.

**Fairy Ring Champignon,
Fairy Ring Marasmius**
(Marasmius oreades)

The cap is bell-shaped when young, changing to convex, then flattening but with an umbo, smooth; the margin striate or wavy; the gills broad, adnexed, widely spaced, which may have smaller gills between. The stem is tough, elastic and slender, and may be scaly or downy at its base. Edible. Much relished by connoisseurs for the caps' pleasant mushroom flavour and fragrant aroma though the stem is tough, but is obviously disliked by greenkeepers and stewards. It can be dried and stored for winter use, as a condiment for soup flavouring.

Colour: cap whitish, pale tan, buff, when moist, may have a pinkish tint, but paler when dry; gills white at first, then creamy or buff; stem as cap or paler; flesh whitish or pale brown; spores white.

Height: up to 4 inches; cap up to $2\frac{1}{2}$ inches in diameter.

Garlic-Scented Marasmius (British Isles) (*Marasmius alliaceus*):

British Isles.

On decaying twigs, sticks, leaves, needles and similar debris, particularly in conifer forests. In small groups. Common. Summer, autumn.

Similar to Fairy Ring Champignon but the convex cap is wrinkled when dry; the margin is striate, the few gills being attached to the slender, shiny stem. Edible. Has a distinct identifying garlic aroma and flavour.

Colour: cap clay-brown, tan, whitish when dry; gills whitish; stem black; spores white.

Height: up to $1\frac{1}{2}$ inches; cap up to 1 inch in diameter.

Garlic Marasmius (North America) (*Marasmius scorodonius*):

British Isles, North America.

In North America, found in same habitats as Garlic-Scented Marasmius, but also occurs in grass in the British Isles. Similar to Garlic-Scented Marasmius. Edible, with a garlic aroma.

Colour: cap dull red, whitish when dry; stem pale reddish, shiny.

Height: up to $1\frac{1}{2}$ inches; cap up to 1 inch in diameter.

Little Wheel Marasmius (North America), Little Wheel Toadstool (British Isles) *(Marasmius rotula):*
British Isles, North America.

Woodlands; on decaying twigs and similar debris. In clusters. Fairly common. Summer, autumn.

The cap has obvious radial furrows on its margin, and a small central depression; there are few gills, which are distant, attached to a collar around the apex of the stem like the spokes of a wheel, a feature which immediately identifies it. The stem is long, thin, stiff and shiny. Edible, but too small to be worthwhile.
Colour: cap dull whitish–grey; gills white; stem black; spores white.
Height: up to 1½ inches; cap up to ½ inch in diameter.

Garlic Marasmius *(Marasmius scorodonius)*

Little Wheel Marasmius, Little Wheel Toadstool *(Marasmius rotula)*

Twig Marasmius *(Marasmius ramealis):*
British Isles.

On decaying twigs, particularly wild rose and bramble. In groups along length of habitat. Common. Summer, autumn.

The cap is flat with a shallow central depression; the gills distant and the stem has a mealy texture, curving from its point of attachment to the habitat.

120

Colour: cap white or pale flesh–pink; gills white; stem white or pale flesh; spores white.
Height: up to 1 inch; cap about ¼ inch in diameter.

Twig Marasmius *(Marasmius ramealis)*

Wood Woolly Foot *(Marasmius [Collybia] peronatus)*

Wood Woolly Foot *(Marasmius [Collybia] peronatus):*
British Isles.

Woodlands, particularly beech; on dead leaves and twig debris. In groups. Very common. Late summer, autumn.

The cap is convex and tough with a margin which may be wrinkled and inrolled; the gills leathery; the stem cartilaginous, thin and long with a curved base clothed thickly with 'woolly' mycelium, the latter usually attaching it to the leaves on the habitat surface. Edible, but hardly palatable, as the flesh has a strong peppery flavour.

Colour: cap purplish-brown, russet-brown or reddish-brown, fades to yellowish-brown as it ages; gills yellowish becoming brown; stem yellowish-brown; mycelium 'wool' pale yellowish; spores white.
Height: up to 3 inches; cap up to 2½ inches in diameter.

MYCENA

The *Mycena* is a large genus related to *Collybia*, but its cap margins are straight, never incurved, the thin gills being

121

adnate or adnexed, not decurrent. Most species are small, with thin, striated, bell-shaped or conical caps and a cartilaginous stem without ring or volva. For positive identification of some small species examination by hand lens or microscope is essential.

Bleeding Mycena (British Isles, North America), Reddish-Brown Mycena (North America) *(Mycena haematopus):*
British Isles, North America.

On old stumps and logs of broadleafed trees, particularly alder. In clusters, occasionally singly. Fairly common. Late spring to early winter.

The cap is bell-shaped or conical, smooth or with radiating ridges at its margin, the margin itself scalloped or toothed; the gills partly attached to the hollow, brittle stem which if broken exudes a blood-red juice, hence the name. Edible, but not highly valued.

Colour: cap dull greyish-brown or reddish-brown, with a purple tint, margin paler; gills whitish or grey with a pink, reddish or lilac tint, becoming reddish-brown as they age; stem as cap, tinted with red then deep brownish-red or purplish near base; spores white.

Height: up to 3 inches; cap up to 1½ inches in diameter.

Capped Mycena (North America), Grey Bonnet Mycena (British Isles) *(Mycena galericulata):*
British Isles, North America.

On old stumps, wood, and dead leaves. In clusters. Very common. Throughout year if climate suitable.

The cap is conical when young, later flattened; it is smooth and striate with a central umbo. The gills are broad and distant and may be connected by cross-veins, adnate with a decurrent tooth; the stem, slender, tall, tough and elastic, may be curved. It is shiny smooth on its upper portion with hairy mycelium at base. Edible, with a delicate flavour.

Colour: cap, variable, whitish-grey, smoky-brown to pale fawn; gills white becoming pinkish as they age; stem same as cap or silvery-grey; base mycelium white; spores white.

Height: up to 2½ inches; cap up to 2 inches in diameter.

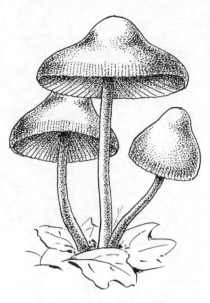

Capped Mycena, Grey Bonnet Mycena *(Mycena galericulata)*

Clean Mycena (North America), Lilac Mycena (British Isles) *(Mycena pura):*

British Isles, North America.

Woodlands; on dead leaves. Singly or in scattered groups. Fairly common. Late spring, summer, autumn, early winter.

The cap, convex when young, becoming flatter, has an umbo; the gills are very broad, and connected by veins; the stem is smooth, shiny, tall, hollow and fragile, hairy or 'woolly' around the base. Of doubtful edibility, may even be poisonous. Has a radish–like aroma when bruised.

Colour: cap rose, lilac or purplish, darker when moist; gills white or with a pink tint; stem as cap; flesh white or pink tinted; spores white.

Height: up to 4 inches; cap up to 3 inches in diameter.

Mycena avenacea:

British Isles.

On lawns, recreation fields, golf courses etc., in short grass. In groups. Common. Late summer, autumn.

The cap is conical and smooth, the margin striate; the gills have a woolly margin and the stem is tough, slender, smooth and shiny.

Colour: cap olive-brown or honey-colour; gills greyish with olive-brown edges; stem as cap but paler at summit; flesh, cap whitish, stem brown; spores white.

Height: up to 2½ inches; cap up to ¾ inch in diameter.

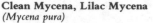

Clean Mycena, Lilac Mycena
(Mycena pura)

Mycena inclinata:

British Isles.

On old tree stumps, particularly oak and sweet chestnut. In clusters. Common. Late summer, autumn.

Very similar to Capped Grey Bonnet Mycena but the stem is yellowish on its upper portion and dark rusty reddish-brown towards and at the base; the cap is also a darker brown. It has a rancid aroma.

Milk Drop Mycena *(Mycena galopus):*

British Isles.

Woodlands; on dead twigs, sticks, small pieces of wood, among needles and leaves. In groups. Common. Late summer, autumn, early winter.

The cap is bell-shaped or conical, striate; the stem fragile, smooth on its upper portion and hairy around base; when

broken the stem exudes a milky-white latex, hence the name. A variety, *candida*, is pure white.
Colour: cap greyish, pale tan, centre darker; gills white or greyish-white; stem grey; spores white.
Height: up to 2 inches; cap up to ½ inch in diameter.

Milk Drop Mycena
(*Mycena galopus*)

Orange Bonnet (*Mycena acicula*)

Orange Bonnet (*Mycena acicula*):
British Isles.

Woodlands; on small twigs, pieces of wood and similar debris. In groups. Common. Late spring, summer, autumn.

The cap is cone-shaped, the gills distant and the stem slender and curving.

Colour: cap orange, with a vermilion tint; gills yellow; stem yellow; spores white.
Height: up to 2 inches; cap up to ½ inch in diameter.

Roof Nail (*Mycena polygramma*):
British Isles.

Woodlands; on stumps of dead trees, logs, fallen branches and similar debris. Fairly common. Summer, autumn.

The conical cap has a distinct umbo. The stem is long, with raised spiral lines and hair around the base.
Colour: cap steel grey; gills greyish–white; stem as cap; spores whitish.
Height: up to 3½ inches; cap up to 1 inch in diameter.

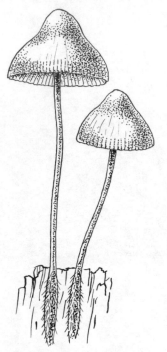

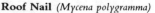

Roof Nail *(Mycena polygramma)*

Umbrella–Like Omphalia
([Omphalia umbellifera] Omphalia ericetorum [Umbellifera])

White Bonnet *(Mycena tenerrima):*
British Isles.

Occurs on trunks of trees and other wood. In scattered groups. Common. Throughout year.

The conical cap is coated with a fine powder giving it a frosted appearance; the gills are crowded, the stem thin and fragile.
Colour: cap, gills, stem and spores, white.
Height: up to 1 inch; cap ¼ inch in diameter.

126

OMPHALIA

The *Omphalia* genus is similar to *Mycena* in having a cartilaginous stem, but the gills are decurrent, not adnate or adnexed. Most of the species are extremely small, uncommon or rare.

Omphalia ericetorum – *Omphalia umbellifera* (British Isles), Umbrella-Like Omphalia (North America)
British Isles, North America.

Heaths, in damp, shady coniferous and mixed woodlands; on decaying wood, moss-covered soil and wet, peaty soil. Singly or in large scattered groups. Fairly common, British Isles, common, North America. Autumn, winter, spring, summer.

The cap is convex when young, later flattening, with a shallow, central depression, radiating furrows which are obvious when wet, and a scalloped margin; the gills are broad, very distant, joined by veins and decurrent; the stem smooth, cartilaginous, slender and solid, hollowing later. Edible.
Colour: cap, variable, whitish, greyish, pale straw, creamy-brown; gills white, then creamy or yellowish; stem as cap; flesh, as cap; spores white.
Height: up to 1 inch; cap up to $\frac{3}{4}$ inch in diameter.

PLEUROTACEAE
Pleurotus

The *Pleurotus* genus does not occur on the ground, living instead on unhealthy trees, stumps, fallen trunks and logs, sometimes at a considerable height. Species are often large and fleshy with an excentric or lateral stem or occasionally none at all. The gills are adnexed or decurrent. *Crepidotus* is now classified with the *Pleurotaceae*, but see *Agaricales–Ochrosporae*.

Angel Wings (North America), Expanded Pleurotus (North America) *(Pleurotus porrigens):*
North America.

On fallen, decaying logs of conifers, also with a liking for hemlock. In small, scattered groups or larger groups. Common. Autumn.

The fan-shaped cap is thin and fragile, sessile, or extended to a stem-like portion, there being no true stem. Smooth above, it is cottony near its base, with inward rolled margins. The gills are narrow and close, a few of them forked near the base. Edible, with a mild flavour and aroma.

Colour: cap, above glistening white; gills white or whitish; flesh and spores white.

Width: up to $3\frac{1}{2}$ inches.

Elm Tree Pleurotus *(Pleurotus ulmarius)*

Elm Tree Pleurotus *(Pleurotus ulmarius):*
British Isles, North America.

On elm trees, occasionally on other hardwoods. Singly or small clusters. Fairly common. Late summer, autumn, early winter.

The cap is convex when young, later flattening; at first firm, it becomes cracked and scaly as it ages. The gills are broad, fairly crowded; the stem thick, solid, firm and usually excentric, being thicker near and at the base. Edible when young, with a pleasant flavour and aroma.

Colour: cap whitish, cream, buff, pale fawn; gills, stem, flesh and spores white.

Height: up to 4 inches; cap up to 6 inches in diameter.

Oyster Mushroom,
Oyster Pleurotus
(Pleurotus ostreatus)

Oyster Mushroom (British Isles), Oyster Pleurotus (North America) *(Pleurotus ostreatus):*

British Isles, North America.

On various living, dying or dead hardwood trees, especially beech: on trunks, branches, stumps, posts, logs. In tight clusters one above another. Common. Late autumn, winter.

The cap is approximately shell–shaped, smooth and moist with a fleshy margin turned downward when young. The gills are broad, distant and very decurrent; the stem, if present, is very short and thick and attached to one side of the cap. Edible, worthwhile when young but tough when mature. Colour: cap steel–blue, grey, or near–black when young, becoming paler, whitish, yellowish, fawn or brown as it ages; gills white when young, becoming yellowish; stem and flesh white; spores whitish or pale lilac in quantity, but separate for microscopic examination they look colourless.

Height: up to 1½ inches; cap up to 6 inches in diameter.

Pleurotus cornucopiae:

British Isles.

On elm trees, fallen trunks and branches. In numerous clusters. Common. Summer, autumn.

Similar to Oyster Mushroom (*Pleurotus ostreatus*) but the cap is more funnel than shell-shaped; the almost central stem is also more clearly defined.

Colour: cap dirty yellow, fawn, or pale brown.

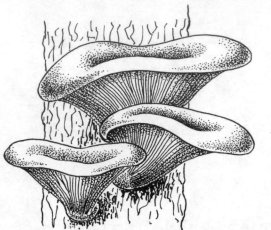

Pleurotus cornucopiae

Pleurotus corticatus:
British Isles.

On trunks of broad-leaved trees. In clusters. Fairly common. Late autumn, winter.

Similar to Elm Tree Pleurotus (*Pleurotus ulmarius*), but the cap has a covering of soft scales, the stem being excentric, short and thick.

Colour: cap greyish-white, cap scales greyish.

Sapid Pleurotus *(Pleurotus sapidus):*
North America.

On dead trees, fallen trunks and branches, stumps and logs. In large clusters. Spring, summer, late autumn. Very like Oyster Mushroom (*Pleurotus ostreatus*); indeed in North America this species is also known as the Oyster Mushroom, thus creating confusion until the facts are studied.

The cap is near-circular, fan or shell-shaped, but usually has a central depression, smooth; the incurved margin may be lobed. The gills are thin, close and very decurrent; the stem, more distinct is near-central or lateral and solid. Edible when young, with a mild flavour.

Colour: cap white, pale tan or brownish; gills white or greyish; stem as cap; flesh white; spores lilac.

Height: up to 2 inches; cap up to 5 inches in diameter.

PANUS

The genus *Panus* has smooth margined untoothed gills, and thus differs from the *Lentinus*. The stem, if present, is central or lateral. There is only one example in the British Isles, *Panus torulosus*, but there are several species in the closely related genus *Panellus*, which also have gills with complete margins and short lateral stems and which in North America are classified as *Panus*. An example of the latter is *Panellus* (British Isles) (*Panus* in North America) *stipticus*.

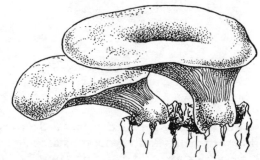

Leathery Panus *(Panus torulosus)*

Leathery Panus (North America) *(Panus torulosus):*
British Isles, North America.

On decaying hardwoods, stumps and logs. Singly or in groups. Fairly common. Spring, summer, autumn.

The cap is rounded when young with an inrolled margin; later broad and flat, and undulating on top. Sometimes funnel-shaped, velvety when young, becoming smooth; gills narrow, very crowded, a few may be forked, very decurrent; stem solid, very excentric, sometimes almost lateral. Edible, but tough and woody. Has a fruity aroma.

Colour: cap flesh with a violet or reddish tint, becoming

yellowish-brown as it ages; gills pale cream or tan, may have a lilac or reddish tint; stem as cap or greyish; flesh whitish; spores white.

Height: up to 2 inches; cap up to 5 inches broad.

PANELLUS

The *Panellus* genus has gills with entire margins and short lateral stems.

Astringent Panus (North America) *(Panellus [Panus] stipticus):*
British Isles, North America.

On decaying hardwood stumps and logs. In clusters, sometimes imbricated. Fairly common. Throughout the year.

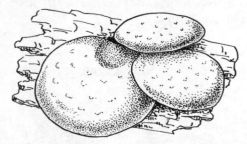

Astringent Panus *(Panellus [Panus] stipticus)*

The kidney-shaped cap has a dry, leathery texture with floury or scurfy scales; the gills are narrow and crowded; the stem very short and growing laterally. Sometimes luminous when wet. Not edible, may be poisonous. Has a very bitter flavour.

Colour; cap pale brown; gills pale brown or cream; stem as cap; spores white.

Height: up to $\frac{1}{2}$ inch; cap up to $1\frac{1}{2}$ inches in diameter.

LENTINUS

The *Lentinus* genus is similar to *Pleurotus* and *Panus,* but has decurrent gills with serrated margins. The stem is excentric or nearly so.

Scaly Lentinus *(Lentinus lepideus):*
British Isles, North America.

On rotting conifer stumps and old posts and railway sleepers despite the creosote. A serious nuisance as the spores penetrate cracks in treated timber beyond the exterior coating of creosote, causing a spreading, crumbling brown wood-rot internally, the sporophore finally growing out from the crevice to continue the destructive process. Singly or in groups. Fairly common. Summer, autumn.

The cap is convex becoming flatter, scaly and fleshy; the gills decurrent and serrated; the stem tough, stout and scaly. Edible when young, becoming tough. The fungus and its habitat have an aroma of liquorice or balsam.

Colour: cap pale fawn, scales brownish; gills white; stem as cap; spores white.

Height: up to 3 inches, cap up to 4 inches in diameter.

LENTINELLUS

The *Lentinellus* genus is separated from the closely related *Lentinus* by having prickly amyloid spores. Only one species is common in the British Isles.

**Common Split Gill,
Common Schizophyllum**
(Schizophyllum commune)

Lentinellus cochleatus:
British Isles.

On hardwood tree stumps. In clusters. Fairly common. Summer, autumn.

The cap is similar to *Lentinus* – fleshy, becoming tough; the gills very decurrent. Has an anise aroma.
Colour: cap pale brown; gills pale brown with a pink tint.
Height: up to 1 inch; cap up to 2 inches in diameter.
The *Schizophyllum* genus is quickly identified by the radiating gills which are split on their free edges. When dry the margin of the cap is rolled back and the halves of the longitudinally split gills twist away from each other. This fungus can survive a long period of dry weather and revive as soon as moistened. The stem is either very short or absent.

Common Split Gill (British Isles), Common Schizophyllum (North America) *(Schizophyllum commune)*:
British Isles, North America.

On hardwood stumps, fallen branches, sawn timber, especially beech; also on imported hardwood. Singly or small groups. Fairly common, southern British Isles, rare elsewhere in British Isles. Summer, autumn.

The kidney or fan-shaped cap is lobed, thin and tough, with very short soft hairs; the split gills radiate from their point of attachment on the sporophore. The stem is absent or very short, when absent the fungus is attached to its habitat by the upper or under surface of the cap.
Colour: cap pale grey when moist, almost white when dry; gills pale greyish-brown with a violet tint; spores white.
Height: up to $\frac{1}{2}$ inch; cap up to $1\frac{1}{2}$ inches wide.

HYGROPHORACEAE

The *Hygrophorus* is a large genus, identified by its characteristic distant, thick, waxy gills. Some specimens are brightly coloured, but none are poisonous and all occur on the ground, in grassy areas or woodland.

Buff Cap (British Isles), Meadow Wax Cap (British Isles), Meadow Hygrophorus (North America) *(Hygrophorus pratensis)*:
British Isles, North America.

Pastureland. Common. Mid-summer, autumn, early winter.

The cap is conical or convex when young, with an umbo, becoming flat or top-shaped in maturity. It is fleshy and dry with margins that sometimes split. The gills, distant and broad are deeply decurrent and may be connected at base; the stem tapers to the base. Edible when young. Has a delicate flavour and pleasant aroma.

Colour: cap pinkish-buff, yellowish or tan, sometimes a reddish tint; gills pale buff, yellowish or white; stem as cap but paler; flesh whitish or buff-coloured; spores white.

Height: up to 3 inches; cap up to 3 inches in diameter.

Buff Cap, Meadow Wax Cap, Meadow Hygrophorus *(Hygrophorus pratensis)*

Conical Hygrophorus, Waxy-Cap Hygrophorus, Conical Wax Cap *(Hygrophorus conicus)*

Conical Hygrophorus (North America) Waxy-Cap Hygrophorus (North America), Conical Wax Cap (British Isles) *(Hygrophorus conicus):*

British Isles, North America.

On grassland, in copses, on heaths, wet mossy stream banks, swampy ground, moist areas in conifer forests. Singly or small groups. Common. Summer, autumn.

The conical, acutely tipped cap is the main identifying feature; otherwise the cap is fleshy, fragile, waxy, and viscid when wet, and if it expands on maturity may split its lobed

135

margin. The gills are waxy, almost free, thin, broad, fairly close, adnexed; the stem very fragile, cylindrical, becoming hollow. Edibility suspect, may be poisonous.

Colour: cap bright scarlet–red, orange–red, orange–yellow, may sometimes have a greenish tint or black streaks; entire fungus may become yellow then black as it ages; blackens when bruised, another identifying factor; gills white, pale yellowish–green to olive, finally blackish; stem as cap, also blackens on being bruised; flesh yellowish–orange, paler than cap; spores white.

Height: up to 4 inches; cap up to 2 inches in diameter.

Golden Wax Cap *(Hygrophorus chlorophanus):*
British Isles.

Pastureland. Singly or in small groups. Fairly common. Autumn.

Similar to *Hygrophorus obrusseus* but smaller and smooth, with an obtuse, viscid cap and a smooth stem.

Colour: entirely chrome yellow.

Cap diameter: up to 2 inches.

Hygrophorus obrusseus

Ivory Wax Cap, Ivory Cap Hygrophorus *(Hygrophorus eburneus)*

136

Hygrophorus nigrescens:

British Isles.

Grassland.

Very similar to Conical Wax Cap (*Hygrophorus conicus*), but the base of stem is white instead of yellow, and also blackens when bruised or cut.

Hygrophorus obrusseus:

British Isles.

In woodlands, on grassland. In small groups. Common. Summer, autumn.

The cap is conical when young, becoming flat; slimy when wet, and fibrillose. The margin curves upwards, usually having several splits. Gills are thick, distant and waxy and the stem thick, often curved.

Colour: cap rich yellow with an orange or olive tint; fibrils orange–brown; gills and stem paler yellow; spores white.

Height: up to 3 inches; cap up to 3 inches in diameter.

Hygrophorus virgineus:

British Isles.

Pastures and downland. Singly or in small groups. Common. Autumn.

The cap is convex when young, then flattened, with a medium height umbo; smooth and dry; the gills are broad, thick, distant and decurrent; the stem solid, slightly tapering towards the base. This species is very similar to Snowy Wax Cap (*Hygrophorus niveus*) and is found in the same habitats, but the latter is smaller, the cap being up to 1 inch in diameter; the cap margin is also striate.

Colour: cap white or ivory; gills white; stem white; flesh, white; spores white. Measures up to 3 inches in height, cap up to 2 inches in diameter.

Ivory Wax Cap (British Isles), Ivory Cap Hygrophorus (North America) *(Hygrophorus eburneus):*

British Isles, North America.

Coniferous and deciduous woodlands, especially on oak. Singly or in small groups. Common. Late summer, autumn.

The cap is convex and umbonate when young, then flat as it

ages; very viscid when wet but shining when dry. The margin is incurved in the early stages and the gills thick and broad, sometimes forked, decurrent; the stem, glutinous over most of its length, has a granular apex and tapers towards the base. It hollows on maturing. Edible, with a pleasant flavour and aroma.

Colour: cap ivory-white, yellowish as it ages; gills, stem, flesh and spores white.

Height: up to 5 inches; cap up to 4 inches in diameter.

Parrot Wax Cap *(Hygrophorus psittacinus):*
British Isles.

Fields, meadows, grassy areas in open woodlands; in short grass. Small groups. Common. Late summer, autumn.

The cap is bell-shaped, then flattened, with a prominent umbo; an identifying factor is that the entire fungus is covered with a greenish slime when young, the cap remaining viscid. The gills are thick, broad, adnate; the stem somewhat slender, but tough.

Colour: entirely greenish when young, later having blue-green and yellow tints, hence its name; cap becomes reddish to pinkish-yellow in areas as it fades and ages.

Height: up to 2 inches; cap up to 1 inch in diameter.

Pinewood Wax Cap *(Hygrophorus hypothejus)*

Scarlet Wax Cap (Hygrophorus *coccineus*)

Pinewood Wax Cap *(Hygrophorus hypothejus):*
British Isles, North America.

In pine woodlands, also peaty boggy areas. Singly. Fairly common. Late autumn, winter.

The cap is top-shaped and flat, with a shallow, central depression, fibrillose and very viscid; the gills waxy, distant and decurrent. The stem is viscid below a transitory ring on the stem.

Colour: cap olive-brown; gills yellow; stem pale olive-brown; spores white.

Height: up to 2 inches; cap up to 1½ inches in diameter.

Snowy Wax Cap *(Hygrophorus niveus)*

Scarlet Wax Cap *(Hygrophorus coccineus):*
British Isles.

In grassy areas near margins of woodlands, also pastures, downland, lawns. In small groups. Common. Summer, autumn, early winter.

The cap is bell-shaped becoming flat, smooth and shiny; the thick, broad and distant gills may be connected by veins and are adnate with a decurrent tooth. The stem is smooth, compressed, not entirely cylindrical, and hollow. Not edible, but harmless.

Colour: cap bright cherry-red or scarlet-red, fading to yellow as it ages; gills yellow or reddish, with a purplish tint at their base; stem scarlet, but base is yellow; flesh is red or yellow; spores white.

139

Height: up to 2½ inches; cap up to 2 inches in diameter.
CRIMSON WAX CAP (*Hygrophorus puniceus*) is closely related but larger, its cap up to 4 inches in diameter and its gills adnexed or almost free from the coarsely fibrous stem. The identifying factor is that this fungus has a white, not yellow, base to the stem.

Vermilion Hygrophorus *(Hygrophorus miniatus):*
North America.
   Open woodlands and on swampy land. In groups. Fairly common. Summer, autumn.
   The cap is flat and dry, and its margin may be lobed and wavy. The gills are distant; the stem slender, smooth and shining. Edible.
Colour: cap bright red, fading to orange as it ages; gills yellow to red; stem scarlet; spores white.
Height: up to 2 inches; cap up to ¾ inch in diameter.

RUSSULACEAE

The *Russula* genus is very large, there being over seventy species in the British Isles and a similar number in North America. It is not difficult to classify a member of the genus *Russula*, as they all have dry, rigid, fragile, brittle gills, granular flesh, no ring and no volva, but some examples are hard to identify within the genus, particularly if they vary considerably in colour. Positive identification may ultimately call for microscopic examination of the spores and the cap's skin. This book therefore describes some of those species that can be identified by sight and taste, with a consideration for the habitat details. Although the majority of the species is considered edible and none is poisonous *when cooked*, only a small portion should be tasted to ascertain flavour. No *Russula* specimen should be tasted *when raw* as blistering of the tongue, mouth and lips may result.

Blackening Russula *(Russula nigricans):*
British Isles, North America.
   Woodlands. Very common. Late summer, autumn.
   From round, the cap flattens with a central depression, and

140

is smooth, solid, and viscid when wet; the margin may be slightly incurved; the gills thick, brittle, unequal in length, and distant; the stem short, thick and solid. Considered edible by some authorities, but the mild flavour becomes slightly acrid later.

Colour: cap cream, dirty white or greyish when young, then sooty-brown, finally black; when cut or bruised, reddish then blackish; gills cream, becoming reddish; stem white; flesh white, red; spores white. Gills, stem and flesh turn almost black when bruised.

Height: up to 2 inches; cap up to 6 inches in diameter.

Blackening Russula
(Russula nigricans)

Black-Purple Russula *(Russula atropurpurea):*
British Isles.

Woodlands. Fairly common. Late summer, autumn.

The cap is smooth, typical of *Russula*; the gills broad and adnexed; the stem changing from firm to spongy. The fungus is immediately recognizable by its coloration. Edible, with a mild flavour.

Colour: cap dark reddish-purple, darker, almost to black, in centre, may have yellow spots as it ages; gills white or cream; stem white, with yellowish or rusty-brown at the base, becoming greyish as it ages; flesh white, then greyish; spores white or pale cream.

Height: up to 3 inches; cap up to 4 inches in diameter.

141

Black-Purple Russula *(Russula atropurpurea)*

Cracked Green Russula *(Russula virescens):*
British Isles, North America.

Deciduous woodlands, especially beech. Fairly common. Summer, autumn.

The cap is convex then flat, sometimes depressed, the surface cuticle is coarsely granular, mealy, and cracks into warty patches, revealing the flesh; the gills are narrow, crowded and forked, and the stem short, stout and firm, tapering to the base. Edible, with a mild flavour.

Colour: cap green, margin paler; gills, stem and flesh white; spores white or pale cream.

Height: up to 2 inches; cap up to 5 inches in diameter.

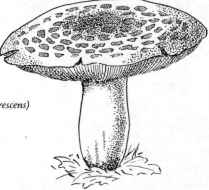

Cracked Green Russula *(Russula virescens)*

142

Emetic Russula (North America), The Sickener (British Isles) *(Russula emetica):*
British Isles, North America.

Coniferous and deciduous woodlands. Singly or in small groups. Common. Summer, autumn.

Immediately recognized by its conspicuous colour. The cap, convex when young, then flattened or depressed, is shiny, with a smooth easily peeled skin that is slightly viscid when wet; the margin is furrowed by radiating lines as it ages. Gills are thin, equal, broad and fairly distant, adnexed or slightly adnate; the stem fragile, either smooth or wrinkled. Inedible. Has a pleasant aroma but a very acrid peppery flavour causing vomiting if eaten raw.

Colour: cap bright red, scarlet rather than purplish, but fading quickly to rosy, pink, yellow or white after heavy rain or as it ages. The gills white; the stem white or tinted pink; flesh white, pinkish under cap skin; spores white.

Height: up to 3 inches; cap up to 3½ inches in diameter.

Emetic Russula, The Sickener
(Russula emetica)

Encrusted Russula *(Russula crustosa):*
North America.

Woodlands and open spaces. Fairly common. Summer, autumn.

The cap is convex when young, then flattened with a cen-

143

tral depression, having small crustlike scales; the margin is furrowed by radiating lines as it ages; the thick stem tapers towards the base. Edible.

Colour: cap tan, with a yellow-green tint; gills, stem and spores white.

Height: up to 2½ inches; cap up to 5 inches in diameter.

Foetid Russula (North America), Stinking Russula (British Isles) *(Russula foetens):*

British Isles, North America.

Woodlands. Fairly common. Summer, autumn.

The cap, convex when young, becomes flat with a central depression; viscid. The margin is striated; the gills fairly crowded, exuding drops of moisture; the stem thick and stout, becoming hollow. Not edible, probably poisonous. It has a strong, foetid, oily aroma and acrid, peppery flavour.

Colour: cap yellow, with a brown or grey hue; gills white or straw, spotted with brown, moisture drops may be red in young specimens; stem white; spores cream.

Height: up to 3 inches; cap up to 5 inches in diameter.

Foetid Russula, Stinking Russula *(Russula foetens)*

Fragile Russula *(Russula fragilis):*

British Isles.

Woodlands. Common. Summer, autumn.

Similar to *Russula emetica*, but smaller. The cap margin is

Plate 9 The **Cep, Edible Boletus** or **King Boletus** (*Boletus edulis*), common in summer and autumn in conifer and broadleafed tree woodlands. Formerly much consumed in Britain and sold in markets, but still retains its popularity in Europe.

Plate 10 An **Earth Star** (*Geastrum fornicatum*). Note how the exoperidium has split into lobes, like legs, to lift the fungus above the habitat.

Plate 11 Some fine examples of the **Shaggy Parasol, Ragged Parasol** or **Shaggy Lepiota** (*Lepiota rhacodes*). They often occur in gardens where there is humus rich soil and compost heaps.

Plate 12 A dense cluster of **Sulphur Tuft** or **Sulphur Top** (*Hypholoma fasciculare*) on the trunk of a dead elm tree.

striate and the gills may have a toothed edge. The stem is spongy, then hollow, and the whole fungus fragile. Not edible. Has a very acrid, peppery flavour, but a pleasant aroma sometimes like pear drop sweets.

Colour: variable; cap typically bright red, central depression being darker, but cap may also have a violet or purplish tint, also be clearly mauve, pinkish-purple, fading to near-white; gills whitish; flesh white, not pink, under cap skin; spores creamy-white.

Height: up to 2 inches; cap up to $2\frac{3}{4}$ inches in diameter.

Golden Russula *(Russula aurata):*
British Isles.

Mixed woodlands. Fairly common. Late summer.

Immediately recognized by its coloration. The cap is typical of *Russula* with an easily peeled skin. Edible, with a mild flavour.

Colour: cap bright orange or brick-red, with golden-yellow areas; gills cream with golden-yellow edges; stem lemon-yellow; flesh lemon-yellow under cap skin; spores white.

Height: up to 3 inches; cap up to 4 inches in diameter.

Milk White Russula *(Russula delica):*
British Isles, North America.

Coniferous and mixed woodland. Singly or in scattered groups. Common. Summer, autumn.

The cap is convex when young, with an incurved margin, then saucer-shaped with a central depression and finally funnel-shaped as it ages; smooth or finely hairy, and dry. The narrow, crowded, decurrent gills alternate long and short, and the stem, short and thick, is cylindric or tapering to base. Edible, but of poor quality; stem has a mild flavour, but the raw gills are acrid.

Colour: cap dull white, occasionally creamy, with rust-brown spots and patches as it ages, may also be adorned by particles of the habitat humus; gills white, occasionally with a pale bluish-green tint on margins close to stem; stem white, bluish-green at summit where gills join; flesh and spores white.

Height: up to 3 inches; cap up to 5 inches in diameter.

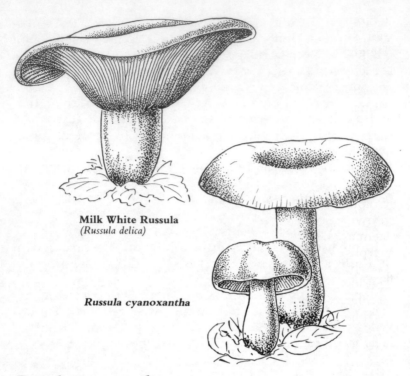

Milk White Russula
(Russula delica)

Russula cyanoxantha

Russula cyanoxantha:
British Isles.

Woodlands. Singly or in scattered groups. Very common. Late summer, autumn.

The typical *Russula* cap has dark radiating markings; the crowded gills are elastic and feel oily when touched. Edible, with a mild flavour.

Colour: variable; cap a mixture of lilac, purple, violet and dark green tints; gills white; stem white, with a purplish tint; spores white.

Height: up to 5 inches; cap up to 5 inches in diameter.

Russula lutea:
British Isles.

Deciduous woodlands. Common. Summer, autumn. Immediately recognised by its colour. Edible, with a mild flavour.

Colour: cap and gills bright egg-yolk yellow, may have a pink tint; stem and flesh white; spores dark cream.
Height: up to 2 inches; cap up to 2 inches in diameter.

Russula sardonia – Russula drimeia:
British Isles.
Coniferous woodlands. Fairly common. Autumn.

The cap is convex with an incurved margin when young, then flat or depressed; smooth and slightly viscid. Gills are narrow and somewhat crowded, adnate; the stem solid and firm. Not edible, being very acrid, but it has a pleasant aroma.
Colour: cap variable, deep violet or bright purple, purplish-brown, darker in the centre; gills citron or sulphur yellow; stem as cap but paler; flesh yellowish, then white, reddish or purplish under cap skin; spores cream.
Height: up to 3 inches; cap up to 4 inches in diameter. This species is not to be confused with *Russula queletii*, also found in coniferous woodlands and which has an umbonate wine-red, purplish or violet cap, turning olive-brown as it ages; gills ivory-white, then creamy-grey; stem as cap; the white flesh has a green tint, but pinkish under cap skin; spores creamy-ochre. Not edible, being very acrid.
Height: up to 3 inches; cap up to 4 inches in diameter.

Yellow Russula *(Russula ochroleuca):*
British Isles, North America.
Woodlands. Often in large groups. Very common. Summer, autumn.

The cap is convex when young, then flattened, with a slight central depression; smooth, slightly viscid when wet. Gills are broad, distant, equal length, adnexed or almost free; the stem is firm, then spongy. Not edible, having an acrid flavour.
Colour: cap yellowish-ochre; gills white; stem white then greyish; flesh white, yellowish under cap skin; spores cream.
Height: up to 3 inches; cap up to 4 inches in diameter. This species is not to be confused with Bright Yellow Russula *(Russula claroflava)*, found in woodlands – chiefly birch – and on boggy ground where sphagnum moss occurs. The cap is a brighter, clear chrome-yellow; the gills yellow, paling as they

age, and stem whitish, pale grey as it ages, and greying where bruised. The spores are cream.
Height: up to 3 inches; cap up to 4 inches in diameter.

Yellow Russula *(Russula ochroleuca)*

LACTARIUS

The genus *Lactarius* is similar to *Russula* in that both have granular, brittle flesh which breaks easily. This breaking immediately distinguishes the genera since *Lactarius* exudes a white or coloured latex, hence its more familiar name of Milk Cap. While some of the genus can be identified positively by sampling this latex – which in several species is acrid, hot and peppery, calling for caution – other species are identified by their odour.

As with *Russula*, definite identification may be possible with some species only after microscopic examination of the spores which are fortunately large.

Lactarius is a large genus, well represented both in the British Isles and North America, thus those species described are readily recognized.

The gills are adnate or decurrent, and there is neither ring nor volva.

Coconut-Scented Milk Cap *(Lactarius glyciosmus):*
British Isles.

Damp birch woodlands, also on wet heaths where there are birches. Common. Autumn.

The cap is flat, covered in minute scales, and has a slight depression in which there is a low, pointed, umbo, the gills are thin, narrow and decurrent, the stem spongy. Not edible. The milk is mild at first, then peppery. Has a strong, sweet aroma of coconut and is not to be confused with *Lactarius mammosus*, which also has an aroma of coconut, but is uncommon, occurring in coniferous woodlands, and is pale brown.

Colour: cap pale greyish with a lilac tint; gills yellowish to flesh; stem pale yellow, tawny-brown if bruised; latex white.
Height: up to 2 inches; cap up to 2½ inches in diameter.

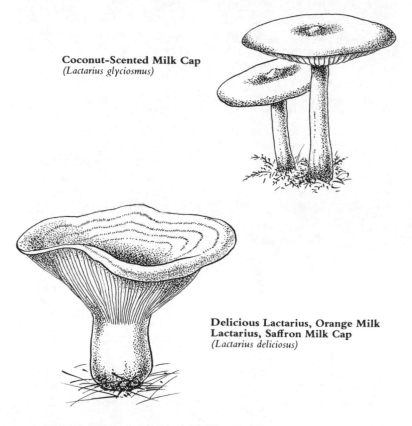

Coconut-Scented Milk Cap
(Lactarius glyciosmus)

Delicious Lactarius, Orange Milk Lactarius, Saffron Milk Cap
(Lactarius deliciosus)

Delicious Lactarius (North America), Orange-Milk Lactarius (North America), Saffron Milk Cap (British Isles) *(Lactarius deliciosus):*

British Isles, North America.

Open conifer and hardwood plantations and parklands. Fairly common. Late summer, autumn.

The cap is convex when young, then either flat with a central depression, or funnel shaped; smooth, having indistinct light and dark concentric zones. The margin may be incurved, later upturned; the gills are thin, narrow, crowded, adnate or decurrent; the stem short, thick and hollow. Edible, with a mild flavour and relished, but turns the urine red for a short time, which may be startling if unexpected!

Colour: cap reddish-orange, orange, pale tan, with green patches as it ages, changing to green where injured; gills saffron-yellow or orange becoming spotted with green as they age; stem orange, also green spotted as it ages or when bruised; flesh white then pinkish to orange finally green; latex saffron or reddish-orange becoming green on exposure; spores pinkish-buff.

Height: up to 4 inches; cap up to 5 inches in diameter.

Fleecy Milk Cap, Velvet Cap
(Lactarius vellereus)

Fleecy Milk Cap, Velvet Cap *(Lactarius vellereus):*

British Isles.

In mixed and broadleafed woodlands. In groups. Common. Autumn.

The funnel-shaped cap is velvety with an incurved margin;

the gills thick and distant and the stem short, very thick. Not edible, the latex being very acrid.

Colour: cap white; gills white then yellowish or pale ochre; stem white perhaps with brown spots as it ages; flesh and latex white.

Height: up to 5 inches; cap up to 10 inches in diameter.

Indigo Lactarius *(Lactarius indigo):*
North America.

Woodlands. Fairly common. Summer, autumn.

Immediately recognized by its coloration. The cap is flat with a central depression, or funnel–shaped; the margin downward curved and lobed. Gills are close set and the stem short and thick. Edible.

Colour: cap indigo with a silvery hue, then grey as it ages; gills, stem and latex dark blue.

Height: up to $2\frac{1}{2}$ inches; cap up to 6 inches in diameter.

Indigo Lactarius *(Lactarius indigo)*

Reddish Lactarius, Rufus Milk Cap *(Lactarius rufus)*

Reddish Lactarius (North America), Rufus Milk Cap (British Isles) *(Lactarius rufus):*
British Isles, North America.

Coniferous woodlands, also boggy, peaty areas. Singly or in small groups. Common. Late summer, autumn, early winter.

The smooth cap is convex when young, with an incurved margin, then flat with a central depression which may form a shallow funnel. The gills are close, may be forked, decurrent; the stem, cylindric and smooth, may be hairy near its base. Not edible, may be poisonous, the latex being very hot, bitter, and peppery.
Colour: cap reddish-brown; gills yellowish becoming completely reddish-yellow or only in blotches as fungus ages; stem paler reddish-brown; flesh pinkish; latex and spores white.
Height: up to 4 inches; cap up to 5 inches in diameter.

Slimy Milk Cap *(Lactarius blennius)*

Slimy Milk Cap *(Lactarius blennius):*
British Isles.

Deciduous woodlands, especially beech. Very common. Late summer, autumn.

The cap is slightly convex when young; then flat with a central depression or alternatively funnel-shaped. It is very slimy, usually having darker concentric spots or markings; its

152

margin is incurved and its gills close, narrow and decurrent. The stem is smooth but slimy. Not edible, the latex having an acrid, peppery flavour.

Colour: cap olive-grey or brown with a greenish tint; gills white, but greyish where bruised; stem grey, paler than cap; flesh white; latex white, becoming grey on exposure; spores pale buff.

Height: up to 2½ inches; cap up to 4 inches in diameter.

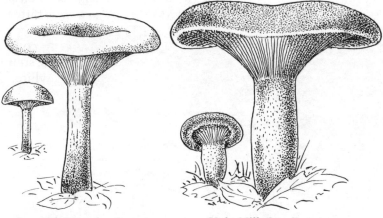

Sweetish Lactarius *(Lactarius subdulcis)*

Ugly Milk Cap *(Lactarius turpis)*

Sweetish Lactarius (North America) *(Lactarius subdulcis):* British Isles, North America.

Mixed woodlands, especially beech. Very common. Late summer, autumn.

The cap is either flat with a central depression or funnel-shaped and its margin may be downward curving and lobed. Gills crowded, narrow, decurrent, and stem smooth. Supposedly edible, but the latex has a slightly bitter flavour and may have an ivy-like aroma.

Colour: cap pale tan or buff with a pinkish or reddish tint; gills buff, sometimes with a flesh tint or near-white, but paler than cap; stem as gills but darkening towards base; flesh as gills; latex white.

Height: up to 3 inches; cap up to 3 inches in diameter.

153

Ugly Milk Cap *(Lactarius turpis):*
British Isles.

On peaty habitats; under or near birch trees. Common. Late summer, autumn.

The flat, slimy cap has a central depression and an inrolled margin, downward curving and hairy; the gills are crowded; the stem short, stout and slimy, with numerous small pits. Not edible, the milk having a very hot, peppery flavour. Colour: cap dark olive-brown, almost black, margin paler or yellow tinted; gills pale straw, brown when bruised; stem dark, as cap; flesh white; latex white.
Height: up to 4 inches; cap up to 6 inches in diameter.

Woolly Milk Cap, Woolly Lactarius *(Lactarius torminosus)*

Woolly Milk Cap (British Isles), Woolly Lactarius (North America) *(Lactarius torminosus):*
British Isles, North America.

Mixed woodlands, on heaths with birch trees, usually on poor soil. Singly or in small groups. Common. Late summer, autumn.

The cap is flat with a central depression, or funnel-shaped, slightly slimy when wet, woolly; the margin incurved and very woolly. Gills are crowded, thin, narrow and decurrent; the stem stout, downy and solid, becoming hollow. Not edible, the milk having a very hot, peppery flavour. Colour: cap strawberry- or flesh-pink, with concentric, pale

154

and dark zones; gills pinkish or flesh tinted; stem as cap; flesh whitish or flesh coloured; latex white; spores pinkish-buff. Height: up to 3 inches; cap up to 4 inches in diameter.

AGARICALES – Rhodosporae

The *Rhodosporae Agaricales* are similar to the *Leucosporae* in form but the spores are definitely a pink, giving a salmon-pink print. The *Rhodosporae* – Pink-Spored Agarics – are sub-divided into three families – the *Rhodophyllaceae*, the *Clitopilaceae* and the *Volvariaceae*.

RHODOPHYLLACEAE

The family *Rhodophyllaceae* has angular, pink spores and is divided into the genera *Entoloma, Leptonia, Eccilia* and *Nolanea*; due to their small size and the need for microscopic identification, the latter two are not described.

ENTOLOMA

The *Entoloma* genus is similar to *Tricholoma*, but has pink, spores rather than white. The cap flesh and fibrous stem are not distinct, the gills are sinuate, and the cap margin is incurved when young.

Livid Entoloma *(Entoloma sinuatum [lividum]):*
British Isles, North America.
   Deciduous woodlands, usually on clay soil. In groups. Not common. Mid-summer, autumn, early winter.
   The cap is convex, becoming flattened, wavy and irregular, smooth with radiating fibrils and has a slight fleshy central boss; the margin is inrolled, then raised. Gills are broad, somewhat distant, sinuate becoming almost free; the flesh thick; the stem thick and striate, may be curved. Poisonous, causing vomiting and diarrhoea, but not usually fatal. Has been mistaken for the Common Field Mushroom. The initial pleasant aroma and flavour of new meal or cucumber soon becomes nauseous.

Colour: cap greyish-fawn, dirty yellow, tawny; gills whitish, yellowish becoming dirty salmon-pink; stem whitish; flesh white; spores dull pink.
Height: up to 5 inches; cap up to 5 inches in diameter.

Livid Entoloma *(Entoloma sinuatum [lividum])*

Leptonia serrulata

LEPTONIA

The small *Leptonia* genus is similar to *Collybia* but has angular pink spores instead of white. There are several species requiring microscopic examination to differentiate, but the following example can be recognized at sight.

Leptonia serrulata:
British Isles, North America.
   Pastureland. Common. Summer, early autumn.
   The cap is convex and fibrillose, shiny when dry; the margin striate, incurved when young. Gills are adnate, with a toothed edge; the stem thin and cartilaginous.
Colour: cap dark steel-blue, blackish-blue; gills bluish-grey becoming flesh pink, gill toothed edge is blackish; stem bluish-grey, summit may have black dots; flesh whitish; spores pink.
Height: up to 3 inches; cap up to 2 inches in diameter.

156

CLITOPILACEAE

The *Clitopilaceae* has pale pink non-angular spores. It is divided into the genera *Clitopilus*, *Lepista* and *Rhodotus*. *Lepista* is similar to *Tricholoma* with which it was formerly included and where it is retained in this book: see Blewits.

CLITOPILUS

The *Clitopilus* genus is similar to *Clitocybe*, but has rosy or salmon-pink spores instead of white.

The Miller *(Clitopilus prunulus):*
British Isles.

In woodland clearings, shady pastures and similar; among grass. In groups. Common. Late summer, autumn.

The cap, which feels like a kid glove, is convex, then flattened, slightly centrally depressed. The margin is inrolled when young, then wavy, mealy; gills thin, narrow, close and deeply decurrent; the stem short, downy and striate, narrowing towards the base; the flesh thick and soft. Edible. The name is derived from its floury colour and, when fresh, the strong aroma of new meal. Not to be confused with the poisonous, white-gilled *Clitocybe*.
Colour: cap pure white; gills white then pale flesh; stem and flesh white; spores salmon-pink.
Height: up to 3 inches; cap up to 4 inches in diameter.

The Miller *(Clitopilus prunulus)*

157

RHODOTUS

There is only one British species in this genus which has spiny, pink spores.

Rhodotus palmatus:
British Isles.

On posts, logs, tree stumps. In groups. Fairly common. Summer, autumn.

The convex cap has a translucent, gelatinous and wrinkled skin, particularly near margin, and sometimes exudes a pinkish liquid glueing neighbouring caps together. Gills sinuate; stem hollow, curved and excentric; the flesh thick and firm. Not edible. Has a pleasant aroma but an astringent flavour.

Colour: cap flesh-pink then apricot; gills paler than cap; stem as gills; spores pink.

Height: up to 2 inches; cap up to 2½ inches in diameter.

VOLVARIACEAE

The *Volvariaceae* has smooth, pink spores. It contains two genera – *Volvariella* and *Pluteus*.

VOLVARIELLA

The *Volvariella* genus has a volva, but no ring.

Handsome Volvaria (North America), Rose–Gilled Grisette (British Isles) *(Volvariella speciosa):*
British Isles, North America.

On compost, rotting grass, straw and similar. Not common. Early summer, autumn.

The cap is bell-shaped when young, becoming flattened, with an umbo; smooth and viscid. Gills are long, broad and free; the stem fibrous, tall, tapering to summit; the volva loose. Resembles Tawny Grisette (*Amanitopsis fulva*), but the gills and spores are different when mature. Considered edible by some authorities, but probably poisonous.

Colour: cap whitish, greyish-brown, darker in centre; gills

and spores deep salmon–pink; stem as cap; volva whitish.
Height: up to 8 inches; cap up to 4 inches in diameter.

Silky Volvaria (North America) *(Volvariella bombycina):*
British Isles, North America.

On rotting hardwood trunks and stumps and wood buried
in humus. Not common. Summer, early autumn.

The cap is cone-shaped, then flattened, silky fibrillose,
sometimes shaggy; the margin may be ragged or split. Gills
free; the stem swollen at base. The long volva sometimes
encloses the majority of the stem. Edible.
Colour: cap white; gills deep, rosy pink; stem as cap; volva
yellowish, whitish; spores deep pink.
Height: up to 8 inches; cap up to 8 inches in diameter.

Silky Volvaria
(Volvariella bombycina)

PLUTEUS

The genus *Pluteus* has neither volva nor ring; the gills are very
free from stem, white when young then becoming pink. The
cap and stem separate readily.

159

Deer Toadstool (British Isles), Deer Mushroom (North America), Fawn Pluteus (British Isles, North America)
(Pluteus cervinus):
British Isles, North America.

On rotting wood, fallen branches, trunks, stumps, sawdust and wood chip heaps, or buried wood. Singly or in groups. Very common. Throughout year.

The cap, broad and bell-shaped when young, later flattens or has a slight umbo; it is streaked with dark radiating fibrils, smooth, kid-like, and slimy when wet. The gills are free, crowded, broad; the stem smooth, solid and fibrillose. Edible. Colour: cap greyish-brown, dark sooty-brown, becoming paler with age; margin may be paler than centre; gills whitish becoming salmon-pink; stem whitish to pale brown with dark streaks of longitudinal fibrils; flesh white; spores flesh-pink.
Height: up to 6 inches; cap up to 4 inches in diameter.

Deer Toadstool, Deer Mushroom, Fawn Pluteus *(Pluteus cervinus)*

AGARICALES – Ochrosporae

The *Ochrosporae agaricales* are similar to previous *Agaricales* in form, but have distinctly brown spores, which excludes brownish-black. The group is very large and it is only possible to describe a few members. The *Ochrosporae* – Brown-Spored

Plate 13 A group of *Pholiota spectabilis*, a striking golden brown species that occurs in tufts on broadleafed and conifer trees and stumps.

Plate 14 The **Common Stinkhorn** or **Wood Witch** (*Phallus impudicus*), which occurs in woodlands and wooded gardens and makes its presence known by its unpleasant aroma, attractive to flies, but repellant to human beings!

Plate 15 The **Fly Agaric** or **Fly Amanita** (*Amanita muscaria*) immediately recognized as the species used in children's fairy tale picture books, but also a poisonous relative of the Death Cap. It was named because it was formerly used in milk as a fly killer.

Plate 16 The edible **Field** or **Meadow Mushroom** (*Agaricus campestris*), traditionally the most popular fungi to consume in Britain. Note its differences with that of the Death Cap in Plate 7.

Agarics – is divided into two families, the *Cortinariaceae* and *Bolbitiaceae*. *Crepidotus*, with brown spores, is also included at the end of the *Ochrosporae*, although it is nowadays classified with the *Pleurotaceae* family.

CORTINARIACEAE

The *Cortinariaceae* is divided into the following genera: *Cortinarius, Tubaria, Gymnopilus, Pholiota, Hebeloma, Inocybe* and *Naucoria*.

CORTINARIUS

The *Cortinarius* genus can be recognized when young by the weblike veil – the cortina – from the stem to the cap margin covering the gills and composed of fine strands of hyphae, but on mature specimens this veil may survive only as a fringe on the cap margin or as a zone of filaments on the stem. The gills are adnate and powdery with rusty-brown spores. The genus is very well represented in the British Isles, with over 300 species, but precise identification of the majority of mature specimens is difficult without microscopic spore examination and the use of chemicals. The following examples, however, should be recognizable in their habitat.

Blood–Red Cortinarius *(Cortinarius sanguineus):*
British Isles.
  Coniferous woodlands. In groups. Common. Late summer, autumn.
  Resembles Red–Gilled Cortinarius. The young cap is silky and fibrillose, later scaly; the gills crowded and adnate; the stem slender, fibrillose. Not edible.
Colour: cap, gills, stem, flesh blood–red; spores rust-brown.
Height: up to 2 inches; cap up to 2 inches in diameter.

Cinnamon Cortinarius *(Cortinarius cinnamomeus):*
British Isles, North America.
  Coniferous woodlands and peaty habitats. Singly or in small groups. Common. Summer, autumn.
  The cap, hemispherical or bell-shaped when young,

becomes semi-flat, umbonate, silky smooth; the gills thin, narrow, adnate; the stem, slender, cylindric and fibrillose, may be solid or hollow. Edible, with a mild flavour but caution is necessary to identify it correctly from species causing illness.

Colour: cap bright yellow-brown, olive-brown to cinnamon-brown; gills yellow then cinnamon–brown; stem pale yellow, olive tinted; flesh pale yellow or tawny; spores rust-brown.
Height: up to 4 inches; cap up to 3 inches in diameter.

Cinnamon Cortinarius
(Cortinarius cinnamomeus)

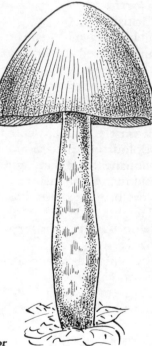

Cortinarius elatior

Cortinarius elatior:
British Isles.

Deciduous woodlands, especially beech and birch. Common. Summer, early autumn.

The cap is bell-shaped then conical, umbonate, slimy, and

radially grooved from middle to margin, which is sometimes lobed. The thick gills are broad, veined, distant, adnate or adnate with a decurrent tooth; the tall stem tapering top and bottom, is slimy and fibrillose, root-like where it enters the habitat. Not edible, but harmless.

Colour: cap yellowish-brown, pale date-brown, may have violet tint, margin paler; gills cinnamon-brown, later reddish-violet; stem whitish, bluish-lilac tinted, zoned by cortina; flesh whitish; spores rust-brown.

Height: up to 6 inches; cap up to 5 inches in diameter.

Cortinarius pholideus:
British Isles.

Under birch trees; on damp, peaty ground. Not uncommon. Summer, autumn.

The cap is bell-shaped then semi-flat, umbonate, with minute, shaggy, recurved scales; gills are thin, crowded, adnate or emarginate; the stem slender and tall, perhaps thicker at the base and shaggy scaled, with a ring-like zone from the remains of the cortina. Not edible, but harmless.

Colour: cap hazel or dark brown; gills violet then cinnamon-brown; stem violet above the ring, brown scaled below it; flesh pale, violet-tinted near stem; spores rust-brown.

Height: up to 5 inches; cap up to 3 inches in diameter.

Red-Gilled Cortinarius (*Cortinarius semisanguineus*)

163

Red–Gilled Cortinarius *(Cortinarius semisanguineus):*
British Isles, North America.

In conifer and birch woodlands, heaths; on wet, peaty ground. Singly or scattered groups. Common. Late summer, autumn.

The cap is convex when young, then broadly rounded, umbonate, smooth and silky; the gills are narrow, crowded and adnate and the stem cylindric, solid and fibrillose, perhaps downy. Edible.

Colour: cap yellowish or olive-brown becoming dark tawny-brown; gills deep blood-red or cinnabar-red, colour changing with light and viewing position; stem yellowish or tawny, with brownish fibrils, downy pinkish-red at stem base; flesh yellowish-white; spores brown.

Height: up to 3 inches; cap up to 3 inches in diameter.

Sheathed Cortinarius *(Cortinarius torvus)*

Violet Cortinarius *(Cortinarius violaceus)*

Sheathed Cortinarius *(Cortinarius torvus):*
British Isles.

Deciduous woodlands, especially beech. Fairly common. Summer, autumn.

164

The cap is convex or bell–shaped, then expanded, umbonate, with silky fibrils when young. The gills are broad, thick, distant, adnate; the stout stem may be curved, but is swollen at the base, the lower portion covered by a stocking–like sheath – the universal veil – which ends in a narrow, membranous ring. The flesh is thick and firm. Not edible, but harmless.

Colour: cap date-brown, violet-brown; gills violet, then dark or rusty-brown; stem whitish, violet-tinted above white ring; sheath whitish; flesh pale, may be violet-tinted; spores rust-brown.

Height: up to 3 inches; cap up to 3 inches in diameter.

Violet Cortinarius (*Cortinarius violaceus*):
British Isles, North America.

Deciduous and coniferous woodlands, especially beech and birch. Singly or small groups. Fairly Common. Late summer, autumn.

The cap is convex when young, then broadly rounded or almost flat, fibrillose and with a metallic appearance when dry; the gills are broad and adnate; the stem, swollen at its base, is silky and may have cortina remnants. Edible, with a mild flavour.

Colour: cap and stem, dark violet; gills violet becoming rust-brown; flesh pale to dark violet; spores rusty cinnamon-brown.

Height: up to 5 inches; cap up to 5 inches in diameter.

TUBARIA

The *Tubaria* genus has decurrent gills, brown spores and a cartilaginous stem.

Scurfy Tubaria (*Tubaria furfuracea*):
British Isles.

In woodlands, on open clearings, by paths, among wood chips and debris, also in fields. In small groups. Common. Throughout year, particularly autumn.

From convex the cap flattens, perhaps with a shallow central depression; it is hygrophanous and mealy, becoming

165

scurfy or hoary when dry and with a striate margin. Gills are distant, slightly decurrent or adnate; the stem slender, hollow and scaly, woolly at the base. Harmless.
Colour: cap reddish-brown when damp, paler when dry; gills cinnamon-brown; stem as cap, base white; flesh pale cinnamon; spores yellowish-brown.
Height: up to 2 inches; cap up to 1 inch in diameter.

Scurfy Tubaria *(Tubaria furfuracea)*

GYMNOPILUS

The gills of the genus *Gymnopilus* are adnate and yellowish to rusty-brown, with rusty-brown spores.

Gymnopilus penetrans *(Flammula sapinea):*
British Isles.

Pine woodlands; on rotting stumps, wood chips where felling took place and on other debris. In small groups. Common. Summer, autumn.

The cap is convex and scaly when young, then flattened and later umbonate. Gills are adnate, broad, thin and crowded; the stem, short, slender and fibrous, may have a cortina zone. Not edible. Has a very acrid flavour.
Colour: cap bright yellowish-orange or tawny-golden, centrally orange-red, margin yellowish; gills yellow when young, then with rusty-brown spots, finally tawny-gold;

stem yellowish; flesh cap yellowish, stem yellowish then rusty-brown; spores rusty-brown.
Height: up to 2 inches; cap up to 3 inches in diameter.

Gymnopilus penetrans *(Flammula sapinea)*

PHOLIOTA

The *Pholiota* genus has adnate or decurrent gills and smooth, rusty-brown spores.

Pholiota [galerina] mutabilis:
British Isles.

On Hardwood trunks, stumps and logs. In crowded tufts. Common. Spring, summer, autumn.

The cap is convex, then flatter, but with an umbo; hygrophanous, smooth or slightly viscid. The slender, firm stem may curve from a vertical habitat, being scaly below its well–developed membranous ring. Edible, with a pleasant flavour.

Colour: cap dark brown when damp, centrally pale brown when dry, with margin darker or whole cap pale; gills pale cinnamon becoming darker; stem brown; scales dark brown; flesh whitish; spores rusty-brown.
Height: up to 2 inches; cap up to 2 inches in diameter.

167

Pholiota [Galerina] mutabilis

Pholiota spectabilis:
British Isles.

On hardwood trunks, stumps and logs. In crowded tufts. Common. Summer, autumn.

The cap is convex then flatter, but umbonate, fibrillose; stem sturdy, thick, ventricose; ring prominent. Edible. Colour: cap golden-yellow; gills yellow; stem paler above ring, as cap, brownish below ring; spores rusty-brown. Height: up to 5 inches; cap up to 4 inches in diameter.

Rough Pholiota (North America), Scaly Pholiota (North America), Shaggy Pholiota (British Isles)
(Pholiota squarrosa):
British Isles, North America.

On the base of coniferous and broadleafed tree trunks, also logs and stumps. In crowded clusters. Common. Summer, autumn, early winter.

When young, the cap is convex and the margin inrolled; it is later rounded or flattened, but with a central umbo, and covered with shaggy, recurved scales; the gills are adnate with a decurrent tooth; the stem long, solid, cylindrical or tapering to the base and sometimes curved; smooth above the ring, and covered with recurved scales below. The ring is small,

168

membranous, and sometimes torn, or absent. Edible. Has a strong, unpleasant aroma but a mild flavour.

Colour: cap yellowish-brown, scales rusty-brown, cap margin may be greenish tinted; gills pale yellow, then greenish-yellow, dark rusty-brown as they age; stem yellowish above ring, below ring rusty-brown; ring dark brown; flesh yellowish; spores rusty-brown.

Height: up to 5 inches; cap up to 4 inches in diameter.

Rough Pholiota, Scaly Pholiota, Shaggy Pholiota *(Pholiota squarrosa)*

Yellow Pholiota (North America), Golden Phaeolepiota (North America) *(Pholiota aurea [Phaeolepiota aurea]):*

North America.

On earth near trees, especially alder. Singly or in groups. Common. Autumn.

When young, the cap is convex, the margin incurved; later, flat or slightly umbonate, with a powdery covering removable when dry. There may be fragments of the veil attached. Gills are broad, crowded, adnate; the stem fibrous, stuffed and powdery coated; the ring membranous and hanging. Edible when young, but only the caps should be eaten. Has a pleasant aroma and mild flavour.

169

Colour: cap pale gold, leather-brown; gills pale yellow then brownish-buff; stem pale above ring, below ring as cap; flesh yellowish; spores pale brown.
Height: up to 12 inches; cap up to 11 inches in diameter.

HEBELOMA

The *Hebeloma* genus has sinuate gills and almond-shaped, dull brown or clay-coloured spores. They are similar in form to the white-spored *Tricholoma* and pink-spored *Entoloma*.

Fairy Cake Hebeloma *(Hebeloma crustuliniforme)*

Fairy Cake Hebeloma *(Hebeloma crustuliniforme):*
British Isles.

In various type woodlands, on heaths, in gardens, where soil is particularly damp. Singly. Common. Late summer, autumn.

The cap is convex and slightly viscid with an inrolled margin, and may have tiny hairs; the gills narrow, crowded and watery, exuding liquid in wet weather. The stem is coarsely powdery at its summit; the flesh firm. Not edible, causing illness. Smells of radishes.
Colour: cap pale tan or whitish-brown; gills greyish then clay-brown; stem whitish-brown, powder white; flesh white; spores dull brown.
Height: up to 3 inches; cap up to 3 inches in diameter.

Hebeloma mesophaeum:
British Isles.

In open clearings in woodlands, particularly where there are numerous birch and pine, also on heaths with these trees. Fairly common. Late summer, autumn, early winter.

The cap is convex, then flattened, slightly viscid; gills when young are covered by a veil which breaks, surviving as a ring on the fibrillose stem. Not edible.

Colour: cap centrally dark brown, margin paler; gills and stem whitish when young then brown; flesh pale brown; spores dull brown.

Height: up to 2 inches; cap up to 2 inches in diameter.

INOCYBE

The *Inocybe* genus has adnate or adnexed gills and dull brown, olive or yellowish–clay spores. The cap is fibrillose, scaly or silky. Some of the small species are difficult to identify without microscopic examination.

White Inocybe, Earth–Leaf Inocybe *(Inocybe geophylla)*

White Inocybe, Earth–Leaf Inocybe (North America)
(Inocybe geophylla):
British Isles, North America.

In open, damp coniferous and mixed woodlands; upon leaves. On grassy areas under conifers. Singly or in small groups. Common. Summer, autumn, early winter.

171

The immature convex cap changes to conical or bell-shaped with a pointed umbo; shiny, silky, smooth. Gills are narrow and close, having a thin veil when young. The stem is cylindrical, solid, smooth and silky, hairy at summit; the flesh thin. Poisonous. Has an earthy aroma.

Colour: cap of typical form is white; gills and stem white, becoming greyish then brown; spores brown. There is, however, a common variety *Inocybe lilacina*, which has a pale lilac cap and stem.

Height: up to 2 inches; cap up to 1 inch in diameter.

Red-Staining Inocybe
(Inocybe patouillardii)

Red-Staining Inocybe *(Inocybe patouillardii):*
British Isles.

Woodland clearings and edges, alongside paths, in grass. Singly or a scattered group. Not common. Spring, summer, sometimes autumn.

The semi-conical cap has a distinct umbo and is dry and silky; the lobed margin may be split. The gills are crowded, emarginate or almost free; the stem solid, smooth, fibrous and the flesh firm. Very poisonous, causing illness or death. Has a fruity aroma. Not to be confused with the edible Field Mushroom or St George's Mushroom.

Colour: cap white or cream when young becoming yellowish then vermilion-red; margin splits pinkish; gills white then yellowish-grey or olive, edged with white, may be red-spotted, stains fingers red when rubbed; stem white, may

172

be pinkish or red spotted if bruised; flesh white, but reddens if cut; spores dull brown.
Height: up to 3 inches; cap up to 3 inches in diameter.

NAUCORIA

The genus *Naucoria* has adnate or adnexed gills and a cartilaginous stem, resembling *Collybia* and *Leptonia* except that its spores are brown.

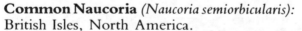

Common Naucoria *(Naucoria semiorbicularis)*

Common Naucoria *(Naucoria semiorbicularis):*
British Isles, North America.
  In grassland. Singly. Common. Summer, early autumn.
  The hemispherical, smooth cap is viscid when wet; gills are crowded and adnate; the slender stem, long, shiny smooth and pithy. Edible.
Colour: cap yellowish; gills cinnamon–brown; stem as cap or tan; flesh whitish; spores dull brown.
Height: up to $2\frac{1}{2}$ inches; cap up to $1\frac{1}{2}$ inches in diameter.

BOLBITIACEAE

The *Bolbitiaceae* is divided into the genera *Bolbitius*, *Conocybe* and *Agrocybe*.

BOLBITIUS

This genus has rusty brown spores and resembles *Coprinus* in that the sporophore liquefies rapidly, yet this is not a method of disposal, the spores having already fallen.

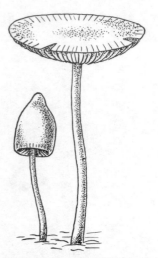

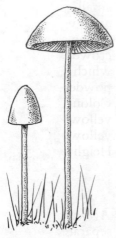

Yellow Cow-Pat Toadstool
(Bolbitius vitellinus)

Brown Cone Cap
(Conocybe tenera)

Yellow Cow-Pat Toadstool *(Bolbitius vitellinus)*:
British Isles.

In well-manured fields and gardens. Singly or in scattered groups. Common. Summer, autumn.

Bell- or acorn-shaped when young, the cap is later umbrella-shaped and finally almost flat, smooth and viscid; the margin is striate and may be split. Gills are broad, thin, crowded and free; the stem slender, hollow, very fragile. The flesh very thin; the spores smooth, with a germ-pore.
Colour: cap egg-yellow; gills cinnamon; stem whitish or yellowish; flesh yellowish; spores yellowish, rusty-brown.
Height: up to 4 inches; cap up to 2 inches in diameter.

CONOCYBE

Members of the genus *Conocybe* have skittle-shaped cystidia on the gills, brown spores with a germ-pore and caps with a powdery surface.

Brown Cone Cap *(Conocybe tenera):*
British Isles.

In fields, by roadsides and paths, on woodland edges or open clearings, among grass, during wet weather. Singly or in small groups. Common. Late spring, summer, autumn, early winter.

The conical cap is finely striate and hygrophanous; the gills crowded and narrow, adnate at first then free from the stem, which is long, straight, slender and striate, with a fine, powdery texture.
Colour: cap rusty yellowish-brown when wet, more yellowish when dry; gills cinnamon-brown; stem as cap; flesh yellowish; spores rusty yellowish-brown.
Height: up to $2\frac{1}{4}$ inches; cap up to $\frac{3}{4}$ inch in diameter.

AGROCYBE

Agrocybe used to be included with *Pholiota*, but has now been separated because its brown spores have clearly defined germ-pores and the cuticle of the cap is cellular.

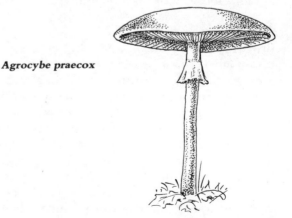

Agrocybe praecox

Agrocybe Praecox:
British Isles.

In woodlands, waste places, along roadside verges, among grass. Common. Spring, summer.

The cap is smooth and fragile; the gills thin and adnate and the stem slender, with a large ring near its summit.
Colour: cap pale ochre, centrally darker; gills dark brown; stem as cap; flesh of cap is white, of stem yellowish-brown; spores brown.
Height: up to 4 inches; cap up to 2 inches in diameter.

Crepidotus variabilis

CREPIDOTUS

This genus is the bracket-shaped Agaric with marginal cystidia and pale or clay-brown spores.

Crepidotus variabilis:
British Isles.

On fallen branches, twigs, and similar wood debris. In groups of several. Common. Throughout year.

The sporophore is round, semi-circular or kidney-shaped, covered with very short hairs and with an incurved margin. The gills are distant, may face upwards; the very short stem is attached laterally to the side of the fruit body, if not absent when the fruit body is secured by its upper surface.
Colour: upper surface greyish-white; gills white becoming pale cinnamon as it ages; spores pale brown.
Width of upper surface: up to 1 inch; height up to $\frac{1}{2}$ inch.

176

Soft Slipper Toadstool *(Crepidotus mollis):*
British Isles.

On dead trunks, logs, stumps. In tiers. Common. Summer, autumn.

The semi-circular or kidney-shaped sporophore is lobed with a thick, gelatinous cuticle, giving the fungus a spongy texture; the gills are crowded and radiating; the very short stem, attached to side of fruit body if not absent.
Colour: cap cream when young, then yellowish-brown; gills pale brown becoming clay-brown, or have brown spots; spores pale brown.
Height: up to 1½ inches; cap up to 2 inches wide.

AGARICALES – Melanosporac

The *Melanosporae Agaricales* are also similar to previous *Agaricales* in form, but have brownish-black, purplish-brown, purplish-black or black spores, not true brown coloured spores. The *Melanosporae* – Black-, Purplish-Black- and Purplish-Brown-Spored Agarics – are divided into four families: *Gomphidiaceae, Strophariaceae, Coprinaceae,* and *Agaricaceae.*

GOMPHIDIACEAE

The small *Gomphidius* genus has distant, decurrent gills and fusiform, very long, black spores. It also has a cortina-like partial veil while young and is similar in form to *Hygrophorus,* with waxy gills, but its spores are a different colour.

Gomphidius rutilus [Gomphidius viscidus]:
British Isles.

Coniferous woodlands; on ground. Singly. Common. Autumn.

The cap is bell-shaped and fleshy, with a prominent umbo, very viscid when wet; gills are waxy, thick, broad, distant, deeply decurrent and the stem solid and tapered. Harmless.
Colour: cap dull brown; margin purplish; gills brownish then dull purple; stem yellowish streaked with purple; flesh yellowish-brown, reddish-yellow or tan, but darker at stem base; spores blackish-olive.

177

Height: up to 4 inches; cap up to 4 inches in diameter.

Peg-Top Gomphidius (North America) *(Gomphidius glutinosus)*:
British Isles, North America.
   Coniferous woodlands; on ground. Singly. Common. Late summer, autumn.

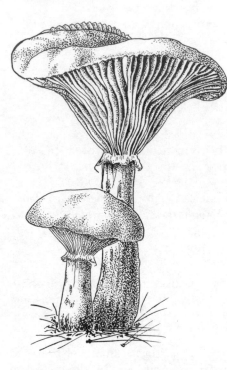

Peg-Top Gomphidius
(Gomphidius glutinosus)

   The convex cap turns top-shaped, fleshy, smooth and so thickly viscid that glutin can be removed in a sheet when wet; the waxy gills are distant and decurrent, with a veil remnant nearby. The stem is solid and tapered, the flesh thick. Edible, but when raw has an acrid flavour.
Colour: cap greyish-brown with a violet tint, old or damaged specimens may be dark spotted; gills pale then grey and blackish; stem pale brown, base yellow; flesh pale in cap, yellow at stem base; spores blackish.
Height: up to 4 inches; cap up to 4 inches in diameter.

STROPHARIACEAE

The *Strophariaceae* is divided into three genera – *Stropharia*, *Hypholoma* and *Psilocybe*.

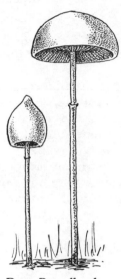

Dung Roundhead
(Stropharia semiglobata)

Verdigris Agaric *(Stropharia aeruginosa)*

STROPHARIA

This genus is similar to *Agaricus*, usually having a membranous ring surviving on the stem, and blackish-brown spores which take on a violet tint under the microscope, but the gills are never free and in some species the cap is viscid.

Dung Roundhead *(Stropharia semiglobata):*
British Isles.

In fields, grazing pastures, gardens, roadsides or similar suitable habitats, on old horse-dung. Singly or several. Common. Late spring, summer, autumn.

The hemispherical cap is bell–shaped and slimy, the gills

broad, the stem slender and long and the ring thin, with the stem slimy below it.

Colour: cap pale straw-yellow; gills dark chocolate-brown; stem yellow; ring dark; flesh pale yellowish-white; spores dark brown.

Height: up to 2½ inches; cap up to 1 inch in diameter.

Verdigris Agaric *(Stropharia aeruginosa):*
British Isles, North America.

Woodlands, pastures, fields; among grass. Common. Summer, autumn.

Rounded when young the cap then flattens with a central umbo, and is very slimy; the margin scaly at first, but the scales disappearing in maturity. Gills are broad and crowded, adnate; the stem slimy when young, has a membranous ring above which it is smooth and below, scaly. Not edible.

Colour: young cap vivid deep blue-green, pigment being in slimy covering, as this and scales removed by rain, cap becomes dull yellowish-green and scales whitish; gills dark brownish-black; stem paler bluish-green, scales whitish; flesh whitish-green; spores blackish-brown.

Height: up to 3 inches; cap up to 4 inches in diameter.

HYPHOLOMA

This genus is similar to the *Tricholoma*, but the spores of *Hypholoma* are dark. The fibrous stem does not have a true ring but when young there is a fibrillose veil which may survive as a circle of fibres on the stem or cap margin. The gills are sinuate.

Brick-Red Hypholoma, Brick Tuft *(Hypholoma sublateritium):*
British Isles, North America.

On logs, stumps and similar. In clusters. Common. Late autumn.

The cap, convex when young, becomes flattened, its margin perhaps having veil remnants; the long stem may be curved, with a ring-like zone. Edible. Has a slight acrid flavour.

Colour: cap brick-red, margin paler; gills yellowish becoming

purplish-brown; stem yellowish; flesh pale yellow; spores purplish-black.
Height: up to 5 inches; cap up to 4 inches in diameter.

**Brick-Red Hypholoma,
Brick Tuft** *(Hypholoma
sublateritium)*

Sulphur Tuft *(Hypholoma
fasciculare)*

Sulphur Tuft (British Isles), Sulphur Top (North America), Tufted Yellow Hypholoma *(Hypholoma fasciculare)*:
British Isles, North America.

On old tree stumps, logs, etc., or from buried wood. In dense clusters. Very common. Throughout year, except in frost.

The young convex cap becomes flattened and smooth; the margin incurved when young, may have veil remnants. Gills are broad, crowded, sinuate; the stem long, slender, hollow and fibrillose, curving from base. Not edible. Has a very acrid flavour.
Colour: cap pale sulphur- or lemon-yellow, centre darker; gills yellow, then olive or greenish-brown; stem and flesh yellow; spores violet-black.
Height: up to 5 inches; cap up to 2 inches in diameter.

PSILOCYBE

The *Psilocybe*. genus contains Agarics with a cartilaginous stem, the cap when young having an incurved margin, the spores being brownish-black or dark purple.

Liberty Cap *(Psilocybe semilanceata)*

Liberty Cap *(Psilocybe semilanceata):*
British Isles.

In fields, on heaths, roadside verges, among grass. In groups. Common. Late summer, autumn.

The cap resembles the Cap of Liberty, the symbol of the French Republic, hence its name; conical, pointed top, with a distinct apical cusp, smooth and may be slimy; the margin pleated and incurved; gills narrow, adnate or adnexed, and the slender, long, tough stem may be waved. Not edible.
Colour: cap pale buff, clay-coloured when dry, darker when wet; gills purplish-brown then blackish, with a white edge or mottled; stem paler than cap, whitish at summit; flesh white; spores blackish.
Height: up to 1 inch; cap up to $\frac{1}{2}$ inch in diameter.

COPRINACEAE

The *Coprinaceae* is divided into four genera – *Coprinus*, *Psathyrella*, *Lacrymaria* and *Panaeolus*.

COPRINUS

This genus contains the well-known fungi called Ink Caps. The gills, which are parallel-sided in section rather than wedge-shaped, undergo a 'self-digestion' in the majority of species, when they liquefy on maturing, forming a black fluid – hence their name – allowing the release of the ripe, black spores. This liquefaction is gradual from the margin upwards, continuing inward to the stem, until the cap is reduced entirely to fluid and eventually only the stem remains. Some specimens may complete the process within a few hours.

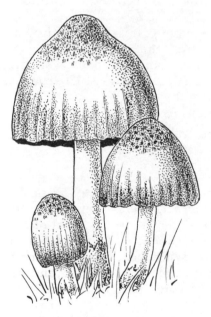

Dungheap Ink Cap *(Coprinus cinereus)*

Common Ink Cap, Inky Coprinus *(Coprinus atramentarius)*

Common Ink Cap, Inky Coprinus (North America)
(Coprinus atramentarius):
British Isles, North America.

In grassy places, alongside woodland paths, near trees, roadside verges, waste ground, also in gardens. In clusters. Common. Late summer, autumn.

The bell-shaped or broad, conical cap is fleshy and centrally scaled; the radially grooved margin may be irregular, lobed or

183

split; the gills broad, crowded and free and the smooth stem tapering to its summit from a ring-like area near the base. Edible when young before beginning 'self-digestion'. Should not be eaten with alcohol as the reaction causes nausea.

Colour: cap pale grey, brownish near summit; gills greyish-white, dark grey, then black; stem white; flesh greyish; spores black.

Height: up to 8 inches; cap up to 3 inches in diameter.

Dungheap Ink Cap *(Coprinus cinereus):*
British Isles.

Dung and manure heaps. In small groups. Common. Throughout year.

The conical cap is scaly when young, but the scales drop in maturity, except from the centre, which may survive even after the cap margin and gills have liquefied. Several stems, swollen at their base, may be united in the habitat. This species also has a root-like extension to the stem.

Colour: cap grey; scales whitish-brown; stem and gills grey.

Height: up to 4 inches; cap up to 1½ inches in diameter.

Glistening Ink Cap *(Coprinus micaceus):*
British Isles, North America.

On or around stumps of various trees, decaying posts, buried wood and similar. In dense clusters. Common. Late spring, summer, late autumn.

The bell-shaped cap is deeply striated and sprinkled with mica-like particles that glisten when young and disappear later. The gills do not entirely liquefy. The stem is thickly covered with very short, stiff hairs. Edible. Has a mild flavour.

Colour: cap yellowish-brown or date-brown; gills dark brown, stem white; spores black.

Height: up to 3 inches; cap up to 2 inches in diameter.

Shaggy Ink Cap (British Isles), Shaggy Mane (North America) *(Coprinus comatus):*
British Isles, North America.

In fields, on disturbed ground, on tennis courts and lawns laid over made-up ground, also on rubbish tips and roadside dumps where wood debris has been buried. In groups. Common. Late spring, summer, autumn.

The oval or long barrel-shaped cap has parallel-sides when young, narrower at the base than at the cap centre, becoming bell-shaped with overlapping, shaggy, upturned scales. The margin is split and the gills broad, thin, crowded and free from the stem which is smooth, brittle and hollow with a thin, moveable ring when young. This ring sometimes slips to the base, disappearing later. Edible before liquefaction begins. Choice and easily digested.

Colour: cap pure white when young with a yellowish summit, then brownish; scales white when young, becoming pinkish at margin then black as 'self-digestion' takes place; gills white, becoming pink then black; stem creamy-white; flesh white or pinkish; spores black.

Height: up to 10 inches; cap up to 3 inches in diameter.

Shaggy Ink Cap, Shaggy Mane
(Coprinus comatus)

PSATHYRELLA

The *Psathyrella* genus has conical, usually striate, caps with dark brownish or black, smooth spores. Most of the species are small and very frail.

Common Psathyrella (North America), Crumble Cap (British Isles) *(Psathyrella [Coprinus] disseminata):*
British Isles, North America.

Mixed woodland, on or around tree stumps. In dense clusters, sometimes in large numbers. Very common. Late spring, summer, autumn.

The bell- or thimble-shaped cap with its rounded summit is very thin, radially striate, deeply grooved and hygrophanous, its gills narrow, crowded and adnate; after shedding its spores this fungus shrivels rather than liquefies. Its thin stem may be curved or wavy. Edible.

Colour: cap yellowish-brown, then greyish, excepting central area; gills white becoming pale and dark grey; stem whitish, almost translucent; flesh white; spores black.

Height: up to 1½ inches; cap up to ½ inch in diameter.

Common Psathyrella, Crumble Cap
(Psathyrella [Coprinus] disseminata)

Graceful Brittle Cap *(Psathyrella gracilis)*

Graceful Brittle Cap *(Psathyrella gracilis):*
British Isles.

In mixed woodlands; among leaves, sticks and other debris.
Singly or in small groups. Common. Late summer, autumn.

The cap is conical and radially striate; the margin grooved;
the gills broad and adnate and the long, stiff, slender stem has a
fibrillose root–like extension into the habitat.
Colour: cap dark brown when wet, pale tan when dry; gills
pale brown, the edges being pink; stem white; spores dark
brownish.
Height: up to 2½ inches; cap up to 1 inch in diameter.

LACRYMARIA

The *Lacrymaria* genus consists of one species that was
previously included in the *Hypholoma*, but is now separated
because it has large, warty spores and is found on the ground,
not in tufts upon tree stumps.

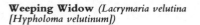

Weeping Widow *(Lacrymaria velutina*
[Hypholoma velutinum])

Weeping Widow *(Lacrymaria velutina [Hypholoma*
velutinum]):
British Isles.

Grassy areas. Singly or in groups. Common. Summer,
autumn.

The cap is bell-shaped, becoming flattened and slightly umbonate, with woolly fibrils forming a marginal fringe when young. Gills are broad, crowded, adnexed or adnate, exuding drops of liquid hence its name, while the long stem is scaly or covered with fibrils. The fibrillose veil of the young fungus may survive as a zone on the mature stem. Edible. Colour: cap, variable, dull clay-brown to ochre-brown, but sometimes orange; gills purplish-brown or blackish-brown and white-edged; stem as cap but paler; spores blackish. Height: up to 4½ inches; cap up to 4 inches in diameter.

PANAEOLUS

Members of this genus have smooth bell-shaped or conical caps, the margins of which project beyond the gills. The young gills are mottled because of irregular ripening of the smooth, lemon-shaped black spores, after which they too turn black. All members of the genus are found on dung or manure heaps, and they do not liquefy.

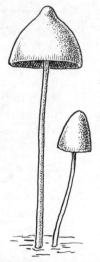

Butterfly Panaeolus
(Panaeolus papilionaceus)

Bell-Shaped Mottle Gill,
Bell-Shaped Panaeolus
(Panaeolus campanulatus)

Bell-Shaped Mottle Gill (British Isles), Bell-Shaped Panaeolus (North America) *(Panaeolus campanulatus):*
British Isles, North America.

On dung and rich soil. In groups of several. Common. Throughout year.

The cap is bell-shaped and smooth with adnate or adnexed, crowded, broad gills and a slender, straight stem with a striate, mealy apex and no ring. Poisonous.
Colour: cap reddish-brown when wet, paler, greyish, shiny when dry; gills mottled, greyish-black; stem reddish-brown; flesh reddish; spores black.
Height: up to 6 inches; cap up to 1 inch in diameter.

Butterfly Panaeolus *(Panaeolus papilionaceus):*
British Isles, North America.

On dung. In groups of several. Common. Throughout year.

With a cap which is either conical and umbonate or a blunt-topped hemisphere, broad gills and a slender, straight or wavy stem with a powdery apex, this fungus is poisonous.
Colour: cap greyish when wet, pale yellowish or clay-coloured when dry; gills mottled, greyish-black; stem pale brown or greyish; spores black.
Height: up to 5 inches; cap up to 1½ inches in diameter.

Panaeolus semiovatus – Anellaria semiovata:
British Isles.

On dung, especially horse droppings. Singly or in groups of several. Very common. Spring, summer, autumn.

The smooth, bell-shaped cap is viscid when wet, shiny when dry; its gills crowded and adnate and its stem straight, with a membranous ring.
Colour: cap pale greyish-brown; gills mottled greyish to black; stem as cap; spores black.
Height: up to 3 inches; cap up to 2 inches in diameter.

AGARICACEAE

The *Agaricaceae* contains the well-known true Mushrooms in the genus *Agaricus*, formerly known as *Psalliota. Agaricus* resembles *Lepiota* with its free gills and conspicuous stem ring, but the spores are dark and smooth. There is no volva. The crowded gills are usually pale, becoming pink, finally a dark purple-brown. The cap and stem separate cleanly and easily.

Bleeding Agaricus *(Agaricus haemorrhoidaria)*

Bleeding Agaricus (North America) *(Agaricus haemorrhoidaria):*
British Isles, North America.

In woodlands, frequently under conifers. Singly. Uncommon. Autumn.

The cap is bell-shaped when young, becoming flatter, but may have an umbo; scaly. The stem is swollen at its base. Edible, but the colour of the flesh may deter would-be consumers.

Colour: cap brown, scales dark brown or grey; gills pale becoming brown; stem white; both flesh and stem become deep red when cut or bruised; spores brown.

Height: up to 4 inches; cap up to 4 inches in diameter.

Field Mushroom (British Isles), Meadow Mushroom (North America) *(Agaricus campestris):*
British Isles, North America.

Pastures, lawns, other grassland. Singly or in scattered groups. Common. Late summer, autumn.

Field Mushroom, Meadow Mushroom
(Agaricus campestris)

The cap is spherical in the button stage, becoming convex and then flatter, with a silky texture. Torn fragments of the partial veil may survive on the margin. The gills are thin, crowded and free, the stem rather short, stout and smooth with a narrow, thin membraneous ring hanging from its upper section, though in later stages it may be absent. It is undeniably edible, and traditionally prized as an excellent, mild flavoured fungus, though the familiar mushroom marketed today is *albida*, a cultivated white form of the wild *Agaricus bisporus* which differs from *A. campestris* by producing only two spores on each basidia, instead of four, as the name suggests.

Colour: cap white or very pale brown – 'mushroom colour'; gills pale pink then bright rose-pink, finally purplish–brown and black as they age; stem white; flesh white, pale pink when cut; spores dark brownish–black.

Height: up to 4 inches; cap up to 5 inches in diameter.

191

Horse Mushroom *(Agarius arvensis)*

Horse Mushroom *(Agaricus arvensis):*
British Isles, North America.

In pastures and fields where horses have grazed, near haystacks, sometimes on lawns. Singly or may be in rings. Fairly common, though less common due to the decline in work horses, though with the revival of interest in pleasure riding, shows and rural sports, the Horse Mushroom may again become as common as the Field Mushroom. Summer, autumn.

The cap is ball-like when young, then flatter, with the texture of a kid glove. The stem is hollow and stout, thickened or swollen at the base, and its lower portion may be split. The ring is thick, broad and spreading, attached to the upper portion of the stem and with its layer of soft scales or patches on its underside is said to be double. The flesh is firm. Edible. Has an anise aroma and rather strong but pleasant flavour, but should not be confused with the poisonous Yellow-Staining Mushroom *(Agaricus xanthoderma)*.

192

Colour: cap white when young, later yellowish, especially in centre; gills white or dull white then pale pinkish-grey (not bright rose-pink) becoming dark brown or black; stem and ring white; flesh white, but stains brownish-yellow (not pink or reddish) when cut; spores dark purplish-brown.

Height: up to 8 inches; cap up to 8 inches in diameter.

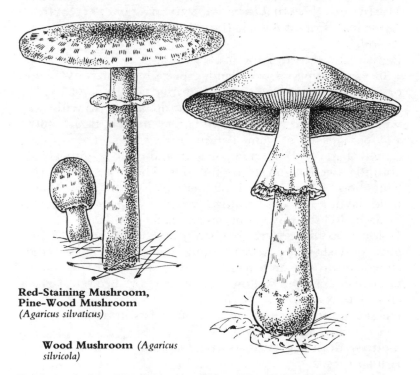

**Red-Staining Mushroom,
Pine-Wood Mushroom**
(Agaricus silvaticus)

Wood Mushroom *(Agaricus
silvicola)*

Red-Staining Mushroom, Pine-Wood Mushroom
(Agaricus silvaticus):
British Isles, North America.

Coniferous woodlands; on needles. Singly. Fairly common. Autumn.

The cap, rounded when young, becomes flatter, with adpressed scales; the stem is slightly swollen at its base with a ring that is prominent but not pendulous. Edible. Choice to eat but the colour of the flesh may be disconcerting.

Colour: cap and scales reddish-brown; gills pink when young

193

becoming reddish-brown; stem white, later reddish-brown; flesh white, but when young becomes pinkish-red or blood-red if bruised or cut, older specimens not reacting in this way; spores chocolate-brown.

Height: up to 4 inches; cap up to 3 inches in diameter.

Wood Mushroom (British Isles, North America), Forest Mushroom (North America), Sylvan agaricus (North America), Forest Agaric (North America) *(Agaricus silvicola):*
British Isles, North America.

In varied types of woodland, especially coniferous. Singly or in groups. Common. Late summer, autumn.

Similar to Field Mushroom (*Agaricus campestris*) with a cap which is rounded at first, then flatter; smooth, fleshy, silky, and perhaps with a small number of scales. The gills are crowded and free, the stem smooth and hollow with its base abruptly swollen and clearly bulbous. The large, double ring hangs loosely, its lower layer perhaps lobed. Edible. Has a mild flavour and anise aroma particularly when damaged or bruised. Relished by some, disagreeable to others.

Colour: cap white or cream when young becoming yellowish; gills greyish-white when young becoming pinkish then chocolate-brown or blackish-brown; stem and ring white; flesh pale cream, yellow when cut or bruised; spores chocolate-brown.

Height: up to 6 inches; cap up to 8 inches in diameter.

Yellow-Staining Mushroom *(Agaricus xanthoderma):*
British Isles.

In fields, pastures, downland, parkland and similar grassland areas, also woodland and hedgerows. Singly or scattered, may be in large numbers. Common, sometimes very common. Summer, autumn.

Similar to Horse Mushroom, but smaller. The cap is ball-shaped when young with a flat summit, then convex and finally spread, its texture silky but the centre may have a few small scales. Gills are free and crowded; the stem smooth, shiny and long, with a swollen, bulbous base, and finally hollow; the ring thick and membranous. Poisonous to some, causing unpleasant stomach disorder but not usually fatal, though other people are able to eat it without ill-effect. Has a strong, unpleasant aroma like carbolic or ink, and strong, unpleasant flavour.

Colour: cap white then creamy, scales dark brown or greyish; gills white then pinkish, finally purplish-brown; stem white then brownish below white ring; flesh white. Cap skin and stem show a bright yellow colour when bruised, rubbed or scratched, yellow finally becoming brown; swollen stem base immediately changes to yellow when cut or injured; spores dark purplish-brown.

Height: up to 5 inches; cap up to 4 inches in diameter.

Yellow-Staining Mushroom
(Agaricus xanthoderma)

CANTHARELLACEAE
Cantharellus

The *Cantharellus* genus is a small one, the species having primitive, branching, broad, shallow, decurrent gills that form deep ridges or thick vein-like folds down to the stem, creating a funnel-shaped cap inseparable from the stem. This genus is the link between the Agaric Gill-Fungi and the *Craterellus*, where the hymenium is not on gills but on a smooth surface instead.

Chanterelle *(Cantharellus cibarius):*
British Isles, North America.

Coniferous and mixed woodland. Singly or in groups. Common. Summer, autumn.

The cap is convex when young, then flat and centrally depressed or funnel-shaped, and smooth; the margin thick, incurved, irregular, wavy and considerably lobed; the gills are vein-like, broad, thick, shallow, blunt, decurrent, narrow folded and forked, and often joined. The stem is short and solid, continuous with the cap with no clear demarcation and narrows downwards to where it may be curved at its base.

Chanterelle *(Cantharellus cibarius)*

This fungus is not to be confused with False Chanterelle (*Clitocybe aurantiaca*). Edible. Highly rated in Europe, though it can be tough. Has a pleasant apricot-like aroma as it dries, but this is not discernable to everyone.

Colour: cap, gills and stem egg-yolk yellow, fading with age; flesh whitish to pale yellowish; spores pale ochre or pinkish-buff, but colourless under a microscope.

Height: up to 3 inches; cap up to 4 inches in diameter.

Cantharellus tubiformis:
British Isles.

In mixed woodlands, among leaves. Common. Late autumn. Similar to Chanterelle (*Cantharellus cibarius*) but smaller, the funnel-shaped cap being dark brown and the hollow stem yellowish. Edible.

Clustered Chanterelle *(Cantharellus clavatus):*
North America.

In shady coniferous forest. In large clusters. Common. Autumn.

The cap is convex when young, then funnel-shaped or developed only on one side; the margin irregular and lobed while the long, narrow, forked, ridge-like gills descend to the base of the short, solid stem which has no demarcation line with the cap. Edible. Relished, but tough, and has a mild flavour.
Colour: cap olive-brown becoming dull-brown; margin purple tinted; gills as cap; stem purplish or olive-brown; flesh whitish or greyish; spores ochreous.
Height: up to 2½ inches; cap up to 4 inches in diameter.

CRATERELLUS

The *Craterellus* genus also has only a few species which, like the related *Cantharellus*, have funnel-shaped caps without true gills or veins, the fertile hymenium being smooth or slightly wrinkled on the exterior of the funnel.

Horn of Plenty, Trompette des Morts *(Craterellus cornucopioides)*

Horn of Plenty (British Isles), Trompette des Morts (France) *(Craterellus cornucopioides):*
British Isles, North America.

Deciduous woodlands, especially beech. In groups, sometimes very numerous. Common. Late summer, autumn.

The cap is deeply funnel–shaped, thin, leathery, and scaly in the centre with a wavy margin. The hymenium is smooth or slightly wrinkled; the stem short and fibrous. Edible, despite its funereal appearance which gave rise to its French name. Has a mild flavour and pleasant aroma.

Colour: cap dark brown, blackish–brown when wet, paler when dry; hymenium greyish–black; stem blackish; spores white.

Height: up to 3 inches; cap up to 4 inches in diameter.

BOLETACEAE

Most of the very large *Boletaceae* group of the *Basidiomycetes* do not have radiating gills on the underside of the cap, having instead a spongy, porous tissue, bearing the spores on the inside of small crowded tubes that open by pores: these are known as Pore Fungi, and their tissue can usually be separated from the cap. The *Boletaceae* are divided into eight genera – *Paxillus, Strobilomyces, Gyroporus, Boletus, Tylopilus, Porphyrellus, Gyrodon* and *Boletinus*, but since the last three are uncommon, they are omitted.

PAXILLUS

This genus, contrary to the true *Boletes*, does have gills, but as these can be separated easily from the cap flesh the genus has been placed in the *Boletaceae*, as opposed to the *Agaricaceae*, although some authorities consider it a genus between the two groups.

Inrolled Paxillus (North America) *(Paxillus involutus):*
British Isles, North America.

Coniferous and mixed woodlands, especially birch. Singly but often in large, scattered numbers. Very common. Late summer, autumn.

The cap is convex when young, then flat and centrally depressed and slightly viscid when moist. The margin, inrolled when young, is grooved, with a hairy fringe; the gills, thin, narrow, very crowded and decurrent, may be joined close to the stem to form a network; the stem itself is short, thicker towards its summit. Edible when cooked, but has a sour taste; poisonous raw.

Colour: cap dull yellowish-brown, may be olive-tinted; gills yellowish, brown-spotted on maturing; stem yellowish-brown with dark brown streaks; flesh yellowish-brown becoming brownish-red when cut or bruised; spores as flesh.

Height: up to 3 inches; cap up to 4 inches in diameter.

Inrolled Paxillus
(Paxillus involutus)

STROBILOMYCES

Only one species of *Strobilomyces* occurs in the British Isles.

Pine Cone Fungus (North America) *(Strobilomyces floccopus [Strobilaceus]):*
British Isles, North America.

Broadleafed woodlands. Not common. Summer, autumn.

Immediately recognized by its cap, near-spherical when young, then flatter, with large, tufty, heavy scales on its entire surface and over the margin, thus resembling a pine cone. The pores are polygonal and wide; the stem long, and may have a pale ring. Not edible, flesh tough.

Colour: cap grey, dark greyish–brown as it ages; scales dark brown; pores greyish, becoming blackish–red if bruised; stem greyish–brown; flesh white, becoming reddish then blackish when bruised.

Height: up to 4 inches; cap up to 4 inches in diameter.

GYROPORUS

Only two species of *Gyroporus* occur in the British Isles.

Pine Cone Fungus *(Strobilomyces floccopus [Strobilaceus])*

Gyroporus castaneus:
British Isles.

Oak woodlands. Fairly common. Summer, autumn.

The cap is velvety with short tubes and pores with rounded entrances; spores round.

Colour: cap chestnut–brown; pores cream; stem as cap; flesh white.

Height: up to 3 inches; cap up to 3 inches in diameter.

The other species, *Gyroporus cyanescens*, is similar but the flesh and spores become dark blue if broken or bruised, as do some species of *Boletus*.

200

BOLETUS

This genus has a large number of species, most of which are soft and fleshy and soon decay. A *Boletus* is easy to classify, but it is not so easy to identify all the species within the genus without microscopic examination, although those described here are recognizable on sight. The flesh of several species changes colour when cut, blue being a possible indication of poison, though none of the species is fatal – indeed, while some are very bitter and unpalatable, others are relished by fungus gourmets.

Boletus bovinus:
British Isles.

Woodlands and heaths; under pine trees. Fairly common. Late summer, autumn.

The cap is slimy and smooth with decurrent tubes and large, angular pores; the stem tapers to its base. Has a strong fruity aroma.

Colour: cap pale brown, buff with a red tint, reddish-brown, sometimes reddish-yellow; margin white when young; tubes yellow then olive-brown as they age; stem yellowish; flesh yellowish, pink tinted.

Height: up to 4 inches; cap up to 4 inches in diameter.

Boletus parasiticus

Boletus parasiticus:
British Isles.

Occurs as a parasite on Earth Balls, particularly *Scleroderma vulgare*, which immediately identifies it. Fairly common. Late summer, autumn.

The cap is rounded and velvety, its surface sometimes cracked; the tubes are short and the stem often curved.

Colour: cap olive-yellow or brownish-yellow; tubes and pores golden-yellow and may have red blotches; stem yellow, sometimes red streaked; flesh yellow.
Height: up to 2 inches; cap up to 2 inches in diameter.

Boletus variegatus:
British Isles.

Heaths and woodlands, particularly under or near pine trees. Fairly common. Autumn.

The typically shaped cap is identified by its sprinkling of soft, small, granular, dark scales on its summit, and it may be slimy when wet; its pores round; its stem stout and smooth, and may be swollen at the base. Edible, but poor quality; improved if pickled in vinegar.

Colour: cap yellowish-brown; scales dark brown; tubes yellowish-grey becoming olive-brown, may change to pale blue where bruised; pores cinnamon; stem dark yellowish with a red tint at the base; flesh yellow with blue blotches where injured; spores yellowish.
Height: up to 4 inches; cap up to 5 inches in diameter.

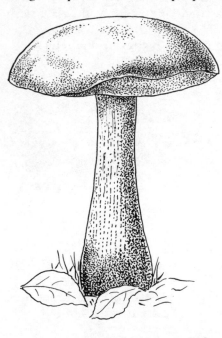

Brown Birch Boletus,
Rough-Stemmed Boletus
(Boletus scaber)

Brown Birch Boletus (British Isles), Rough-Stemmed Boletus (British Isles, North America) *(Boletus scaber):*
British Isles, North America.

In wood and parkland, especially where birch trees are numerous. Singly or in groups. Common. Summer, autumn.

The young convex cap becomes, on maturing, rounded and almost flat, smooth and velvety yet slightly viscid when wet. Its tubes are adnate or almost free, while its thick wart-roughened stem may taper to its summit. Edible: the caps are relished, but the stems are tough. Has a mild flavour and mushroom-like aroma.

Colour: cap, variable – tan, brownish-grey, reddish-brown, dark brown, blackish-brown; tubes whitish then pale brown, but dark brown when bruised; stem whitish with small raised dark or black warts or scales in conspicuous lines; flesh whitish, very faint pale pink or bluish if cut; spores brown. Height: up to 6 inches; cap up to 10 inches in diameter.

Cep, Edible Boletus, King Boletus *(Boletus edulis)*

Cep (British Isles), Edible Boletus (British Isles, North America) King Boletus (North America) *(Boletus edulis):*
British Isles, North America.

Coniferous and broadleafed woodlands. Singly or in scattered groups. Common. Summer, autumn.

The hemispherical cap becomes rounded and flat, looking like a smooth, toasted penny bun. The long, narrow tubes open into small, round pores, while the stem is solid, short and pestle-shaped, sometimes massive. Its close-meshed raised network of white veins covers the upper surface. Edible; highly relished and sold in European markets. Has a nutty flavour and pleasant aroma.

Colour: cap variable, creamy-brown, dark chestnut or tawny, centre darker; tubes and pores white then yellowish-green; stem whitish or pale brown; flesh white with a pink tint, does not change colour when bruised or broken; spores olive-brown or yellowish-brown.

Height: on average up to 6 inches, occasionally 8; cap averages 6 inches in diameter, occasionally up to 12 inches.

Boletus reticulatus is very similar to the Edible Boletus except that it has a granular cap and a stem entirely covered with a close-meshed raised network of white veins. Its spores are also paler, and it is edible.

Devil's Boletus *(Boletus satanas)*:
British Isles.

Under hardwoods, especially beech, and on calcareous soil. Not common. Summer.

The cap hemispherical and thick, with a short, thick stem covered in a network of veins. Poisonous, but not fatal; raw, it causes vomiting. Has a mild flavour and noxious aroma.

Colour: cap pale olive-grey, whitish-grey, greenish-grey; tubes and pores yellow or greenish, then reddish or orange, changing to blue when touched; stem yellowish-brown, yellow on the upper portion; veins reddish, blue when touched; flesh white, bluish-green when cut or bruised.

Height: up to 6 inches; cap up to 8 inches in diameter.

Lurid Boletus *(Boletus luridus)*:
British Isles, North America.

In broadleafed woodlands, on calcareous soil. Not common. Autumn.

The convex, smooth, velvety cap has long tubes; the stem is

thick, with a wide-meshed raised network of veins. Very similar to Red-Stalked Boletus (*Boletus erythropus*) but the tubes of the latter are greenish-yellow. Lurid Boletus pores are blood-red or orange, the stem yellowish-brown stippled with red dots, but the stem does not have the network of veins. When broken the yellow flesh quickly becomes deep blue except at the base of the tubes which stay yellow. Considered edible in the British Isles, with a mild flavour and pleasant aroma, but suspected of being poisonous in North America. Colour: cap, variable, olive-brown, olive-umber, greenish-brown, with a reddish-brown tint; tubes purplish-red at their base; pores bright red, orange-red, maroon; stem yellow, veins red; flesh pale yellow or apricot; entire fungus becomes deep blue on being bruised or cut.

Height: up to 6 inches; cap up to 8 inches in diameter.

Lurid Boletus *(Boletus luridus)*

Red-Cracked Boletus *(Boletus chrysenteron)*

Red–Cracked Boletus *(Boletus chrysenteron):*
British Isles.

In or near broadleafed woodlands; among grass. Very common. Early summer, autumn.

The cap is soft and downy, its skin usually cracked into patches exposing crimson–reddish flesh; the tubes have large, angular pores and the tall stem is fibrous. Edible, mild flavoured.

Colour: cap, variable, purplish-brown, reddish-brown, olive-brownish, fawn; tubes and pores sulphur–yellow, blue when bruised; stem pale yellow, with reddish streaks; flesh pale yellow, except directly beneath the cap skin where it is reddish.

Height: up to 4 inches; cap up to 4 inches in diameter.

Yellow–Cracked Boletus (British Isles, North America)
(Boletus subtomentosus):
British Isles, North America.

Similar to Red-Cracked Boletus and found in the same habitats, but its bright sulphur-yellow tubes and pores become only very faintly blue on being cut or bruised and when the cap skin cracks it reveals yellow flesh.

**Yellow-Brown Boletus,
Brown-Ring Boletus**
(Boletus luterus)

**Yellow-Brown Boletus (North America), Brown-Ring
Boletus (North America)** *(Boletus luterus):*
British Isles, North America.

Coniferous woodlands; among grass. Singly or scattered
groups. Common. Autumn.

The convex, blunt, umbonate cap is fleshy, and very slimy
when wet; the thin, sticky white veil of its youth remains as a
brown ring around the stem. The tubes are short; the pores
small and angular and the short, cylindrical, solid stem is
granulated above the ring. Edible, but not relished due to
slime.

Colour: cap yellow-brown, dull buff, with a violet or greyish
tint from the slime; tubes and pores yellow, then
yellowish-brown; stem pale creamy-yellow, or whitish above
ring, brownish below it; flesh creamy-white or yellowish,
does not change colour when cut or bruised; spores brown.
Height: up to 4 inches; cap up to 5 inches in diameter.

TYLOPILUS

Although closely related to *Boletus* the only British species of
Tylopilus is placed in a separate genus because it has pink
spores and the flesh becomes pink.

Bitter Boletus *(Tylopilus felleus)*

Bitter Boletus *(Tylopilus felleus):*
British Isles.

Deciduous woodlands, especially beech. Fairly common. Summer, autumn.

Similar to Cep (*Boletus edulis*), with a convex, dry, velvety cap and angular pores. The stem has a network of dark brown veins. Not edible. Has a bitter flavour.

Colour: cap pale brown; tubes and pores whitish then pink; stem creamy or brownish; flesh whitish, pink tinted; spores pink.

Height: up to 4 inches; cap up to 4 inches in diameter.

POLYPORACEAE

The *Polyporaceae* group is numerically large and therefore only a few species can be adequately described here. As with *Boletaceae*, the spores are produced in tubes, though the sporophore is not fleshy but corky or woody, forming overlapping brackets in fan, saucer, or hoof-like shapes or lying in clusters on tree trunks or dead wood. Species' height varies down almost to the ground, and an affected tree may carry sporophores for several years.

POLYPORUS

The usually large or conspicuous annual sporophores form clusters, while within the fungi the tube layers are distinct from the flesh and the stems vary from central to lateral and from virtually absent to being fairly long.

Birch Polypore *(Polyporus [Piptoporus] betulinus):*
British Isles.

Only on unhealthy or dead birch timber. Fairly common. Summer.

The sporophore is knob-like when young, later forming a kidney- or hoof-shaped, broad, thick and smooth bracket with an inrolled margin projecting downwards. The pores are small and round; the flesh soft, flexible when young, becoming cork-like. Where this fungus attacks a tree via the

208

cracks in the bark, it causes a reddish–brown crumbling rot in the sapwood and the tree's eventual death.

Colour: upper surface pale greyish–brown, pore surface white; knobs, flesh and spores white.

Width: up to 6 inches.

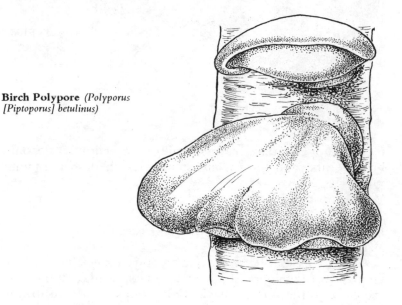

Birch Polypore *(Polyporus [Piptoporus] betulinus)*

Dryad's Saddle *(Polyporus [Melanopus] squamosus):*
British Isles.

On stumps of dead deciduous trees, especially elm and ash, also at various heights on living tree trunks. Usually several close or overlapping. Very common. Late spring, summer, early autumn.

The fan- or saddle-shaped bracket sporophore is depressed in the centre and near the base with adpressed, feathery scales in rough concentric rings. The margin is incurved; the pores large and toothed and the side-growing stem short, thick and stout, reticulated between pores and base. Supposedly edible when young, but later tough and strongly flavoured. Where this fungus attacks living trees it forms a destructive white stringy rot which, at the base of branches can cause them to weaken and crash. Beware when collecting!

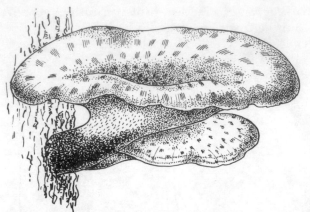

Dryad's Saddle
(Polyporus [Melanopus] squamosus)

Colour: upper surface cream or pale ochre-yellow, scales dark brown; tubes and pores white; stem blackish; flesh and spores white.
Width: up to 14 inches.

Giant Polypore *(Polyporus [Grifola] giganteus):*
British Isles.

Around bases of various hardwoods especially oak and beech, occasionally on soil where roots of dead or dying trees are close to the surface. In tiers or groups. Fairly common. Late summer, autumn, winter.

The fan-shaped sporophore has several smaller fans, each with its own stem, though they merge at the base. The scales are small and fluffy; the tubes short, the pores very small. Edible, but the flesh is fibrous and tough.
Colour: upper surface brown or leather-coloured with a yellow-cream banding around margin; scales brown; pores pale creamy-white, then brownish-red, black when bruised or as they age; flesh as pores; spores colourless.
Width: up to 15 inches.

Sulphur Polypore *(Polyporus [Grifola] sulphureus):*
British Isles, North America.

On stumps, dead branches and trunks, also on living coniferous and deciduous trees. In dense clusters. Fairly common. Late spring, summer, autumn.

210

The sporophore is fan-shaped, with several flat, lobed, tapered, hairy 'fanlets' overlapping each other in tiers from the same stem-like base. Tubes are short; pores minute. The margin is thick and rounded and the fungus will anchor by it when the stem is absent. Edible, but only the tips of young are consumed. The flesh is thick and cheesy, but later too tough, with an acrid flavour and strong but pleasant aroma. In the trees which it attacks it causes a destructive reddish-brown rot in the heartwood so the victim finally becomes hollow.
Colour: upper surface bright sulphur-yellow with orange-red margin when young, becoming orange-yellow, yellowish-tan or dirty white; pore surface pale sulphur-yellow; flesh pale yellow; spores colourless or whitish.
Width: up to 6 inches.

Giant Polypore
(Polyporus [Grifola] giganteus)

Sulphur Polypore
(Polyporus [Grifola] sulphureus)

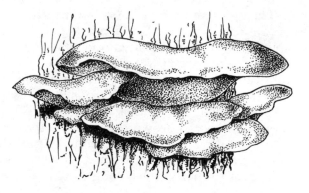

FISTULINA

One species of the genus *Fistulina* occurs in the British Isles and is immediately recognizable by its appearance.

Beef-Steak Fungus (British Isles), Langue de Boeuf (France) *(Fistulina hepatica):*
British Isles, Europe.

**Beef-Steak Fungus,
Langue de Boeuf**
(Fistulina hepatica)

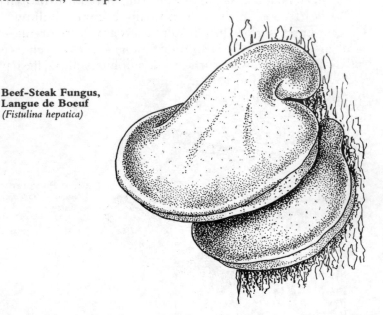

On living tree trunks, especially oak and sweet-chestnut. In a group. Fairly common. Late summer, autumn.

The sporophore is a knob-like protrusion when young, becoming a velvety, broad bracket or 'tongue', hence the aptness of the French name, meaning ox-tongue. The upper surface, slimy when wet, can be moved like human skin; its tubes are short, very narrow and close – like *Boletus* – but not laterally joined. The flesh is fibrous; a short stem occasionally present. Edible, but its thick flesh is slightly acrid with a fruity aroma. It causes a brown rot in the heartwood of its victims, creating dark streaks which eventually give the wood a rich, warm brown hue. This stained timber, known as 'brown oak', was formerly much sought by cabinet makers.

Colour: upper surface dark blood–red, dull crimson, or liver–brown, protrusion at first strawberry; tubes and pores creamy–yellow then rosy–reddish, exuding red drops; flesh purplish, streaked, yielding red juice when cut.
Width: up to 16 inches.

FOMES

This genus has hard and woody perennial sporophores with tubes and pores added in successive layers, and an upper surface distinguished by a crust. Hoof- or bracket-shaped, the genus is reclassified *Ungulina* (hoof-shaped) by some mycologists.

Elm Fomes *(Fomes [Ungulina] ulmarius):*
British Isles.
   On base of elms and on hollow stumps, inside and out. Usually singly or several. Common British Isles, rare Europe.
   The irregular sporophore is bracket-shaped, smooth and lumpy with a swollen, rounded margin and layers of tubes separated by tissue; the pores are minute; the flesh hard and woody. A destructive parasite causing dangerous heart-rot in victims.

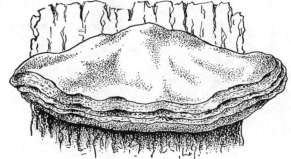

Elm Fomes
(Fomes [Ungulina] ulmarius)

Colour: upper surface whitish–cream, buff; tubes reddish-brown; pores brick-red, orange-brown; flesh white, pale yellow; spores white.
Width: average up to 18 inches, but some specimens may be larger. Not to be confused with
FOMES [UNGULINA] ANNOSUS, common at or just above ground level on standing conifers and deciduous trees,

or felled timber, where it causes destructive heart-rot damage, particularly to spruce. The upper surface of the sporophore is a knobby, velvety, pale brown, later a reddish-brown; margin whitish, tubes yellowish-white, pore surface whitish or cream; flesh woody, white; spores white.

Rusty-Hoof Fomes *(Fomes [Ungulina] fomentarius):*
British Isles, North America, Europe.

On hardwoods, especially beech and birch. Singly or several on victim. Specimens have been known to continue adding pore layers annually for thirty years. Common North America, very rare England, occasional Scotland, very common Europe. Throughout year.

The woody sporophore is hoof-shaped, with fibrous flesh formerly used as tinder.
Colour: sporophore crust greyish or blackish; fleshy tawny.
Width: up to 12 inches in old specimens.

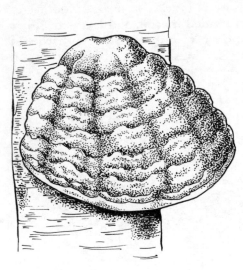

Rusty-Hoof Fomes *(Fomes [Ungulina] fomentarius)*

POLYSTICTUS

Members of this genus have silky or hairy upper surfaces to their leathery sporophores, while underneath the tubes are homogeneous with the flesh.

214

Fir Polystictus *(Polystictus [Coriolus] abietinus):*
British Isles, North America.

On conifers, and their stumps and debris. In overlapping tiers. Common. Throughout year.

The flexible sporophore is a shell-shaped bracket with a hairy upper surface, sometimes narrow, the pores of which have spiked teeth. This fungus causes white honeycomb rot in sapwood.

Colour: upper surface grey; pore surface violet, lilac fading to greyish.

Width: up to 1 inch.

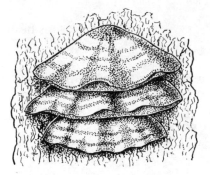

Fir Polystictus *(Polystictus [Coriolus] abietinus)*

Multi-Zoned Polystictus
(Polystictus [Coriolus] versicolor)

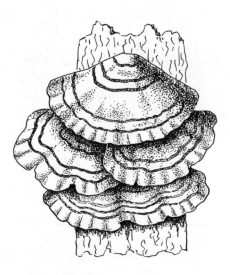

Multi-Zoned Polystictus *(Polystictus [Coriolus] versicolor):*
British Isles, North America.

On hardwoods, their stumps and debris. In overlapping tiers. Very common. Throughout year.

The flat, thin, tough, leathery sporophore is a semi-circular bracket, sometimes imbricated, with a silky upper surface. The pores are minutely round, becoming larger. This fungus causes white rot.

Colour: variable – grey, yellowish, brown or blackish zones in concentric bands; in shady or dark places may be near-white; margin paler; tubes and pores whitish or cream; flesh white; spores cream.

Width: up to 4 inches.

TRAMETES

The species in this large genus are similar to *Polystictus,* except that they are thicker, corky or woody, and usually with larger pores. *Trametes* and the following *Daedalea* and *Lenzites* have been re-classified by several mycologists to the confusion of the amateur, thus it is essential that each factor is noted for positive identification.

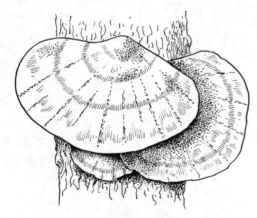

Blushing Trametes
(Trametes rubescens)

Blushing Trametes *(Trametes rubescens):*
British Isles.

On dead branches of hardwoods, especially birch and

216

willow. Singly or several on habitat. Common. Throughout year.

The sporophore is semi-circular, flat, bracket-shaped and wrinkled and zoned concentrically; the pores are rectangular, medium-sized or elongated radially and attached by a broad base; the flesh corky. Causes white rot.

Colour: greyish with a pink tint then reddish-brown; pore surface white or greyish, purple-reddish if bruised; flesh whitish, then pinkish-red, brownish; spores colourless.

Width: up to 4 inches.

Trametes gibbosa:
British Isles.

On hardwood stumps, especially beech. In tiers. Very common. Throughout year.

Similar to *Trametes rubescens* but usually with greenish algae zones on its hairy greyish–white zoned upper surface, this fungus has a blunt, wavy margin, and whitish, radially elongated pores, which do not redden if bruised. Causes white rot.

Width: up to 6 inches.

DAEDALEA

The species of *Daedalea* are very similar to *Trametes* but have spores on a maze-like hymenium, with irregular wavy pores.

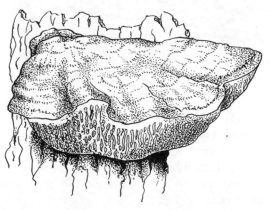

Oak Daedalea *(Daedalea [Trametes] quercina)*

217

Oak Daedalea *(Daedalea [Trametes] quercina):*
British Isles, North America.

On dead wood of oak, beech and other trees, including occasional sweet chestnut; also on their debris. Sometimes on living oak. Very common. Throughout the year.

The hoof- or bracket-shaped sporophore is very tough, woody and uneven, radially wrinkled with concentric furrows and a blunt margin. The tubes are deep; the pores irregular, elongated, wavy and labrynth-like; the flesh corky. Causes a reddish-brown crumbling rot.

Colour: upper surface pale brown or grey; tubes and pores pale brown; flesh greyish-fawn or pale cream; spores colourless.

Width: up to 8 inches.

LENZITES

The *Lenzites* genus is also very similar to *Trametes* and *Daedalea*, but has spores on a hymenium on branching gill-like plates which may be linked to create pore-like chambers.

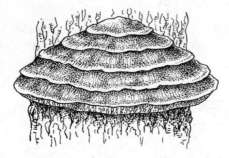

Birch Lenzites *(Lenzites [Trametes] betulina)*

Birch Lenzites *(Lenzites [Trametes] betulina):*
British Isles, North America.

On hardwoods and their debris. In tiers or clusters. Common. Throughout year.

The sporophore is bracket-shaped, hairy and woody; the flesh corky.

Colour: upper surface pale greyish-brown, with light and dark zones; radiating gill–like plates dingy white or yellowish-grey; flesh pale; spores colourless.
Width: up to 4 inches.

HYDNACEAE

The *Hydnaceae* or *Tooth fungus* has the spore-bearing hymenium on spores or growths. There are two forms: one with the typical cap and stem, with tooth-like, pendant spines on the cap underside; the other without a cap, the spines or granular growths developing upon a skin-like or plate-like sporophore.

Common Hydnum (British Isles), Repand Hydnum (North America), Yellow Spine Fungus (North America), Wood Hedgehog (British Isles, North America) *(Hydnum repandum):*
British Isles, North America.

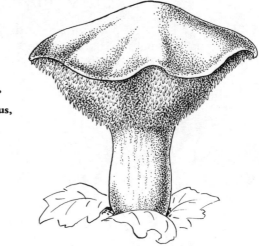

Common Hydnum, Repand Hydnum, Yellow Spine Fungus, Wood Hedgehog
(Hydnum repandum)

Mixed broadleafed woodlands; on the ground. Singly or in groups. Common. Late summer, autumn, early winter.

The sporophore cap is convex or flattened, lobed, thick, fleshy and smooth, with an incurved margin. There are

219

numerous unequal, pointed tooth spines on the cap's underside, that extend down the stem. The stem itself is short, thick and solid, becoming hollow, and may be off-centred. The flesh is firm. Edible when young; mildly acrid.

Colour: cap pinkish-buff, pale yellowish-brown; teeth as cap; stem paler than cap; flesh white.

Height: up to 3 inches; cap up to 5 inches in diameter. A similar species is the

HYDNUM RUFESCENS – also edible – of coniferous woodlands, but this is smaller, with a reddish-brown cap and spines and white or whitish-yellow, tough and acrid flesh.

CLAVARIACEAE

The *Clavariaceae*, the *Club* or *Coral Fungi*, have their smooth, spore-bearing hymenia entirely or partly covering the outer surface of the sporophores, which vary widely in form. The *Clavariaceae* comprises two genera, *Clavaria* and *Sparassis*.

CLAVARIA

This genus has fleshy sporophores, with club-like outgrowths resembling miniature corals, hence its popular name. Coral-like, too, the sporophore may be branched.

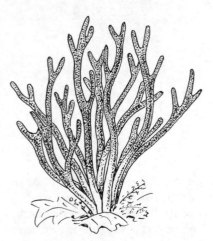

Ashy Coral Fungus *(Clavaria cinerea)*

Ashy Coral Fungus (North America) *(Clavaria cinerea):*
British Isles, North America.

In woodlands; on the ground. In tufts. Very common. Autumn.

The sporophore is variable, but basically erect, irregularly branched, fragile and fleshy; the stalks are fused at their base, sometimes forming a short thick stem; the tips of the branches are blunt, either toothed or flat. Edible.

Colour: whitish–grey with a purplish tint, darkening as it ages; flesh white; spores white.

Height: up to 3 inches.

Clavaria fusiformis:
British Isles.

In fields and pastures among grass, also on open grassy paths in woodlands. In dense tufts. Common. Late summer, autumn.

The unbranched sporophore is spindle-shaped, sharp-pointed, grooved and wavy, with flat clubs. Not edible. Has a bitter flavour.

Colour: bright canary-yellow; club tips may be brown; flesh white or yellowish; spores white.

Height: up to 3 inches.

CLAVARIA VERMICULARIS, dense tufts of which are commonly found in meadows and other grassy places in the early autumn is easily mistaken for *C. fusiformis* (above), but has unbranched, cylindrical and brittle pure white clubs, up to 2 inches tall.

Club Clavaria (North America) *(Clavaria pistillaris):*
British Isles, North America.

Coniferous and mixed woodlands; on damp sites among moss. Not common, British Isles. Late summer, autumn.

The single, unbranched, club-shaped sporophore tapers downwards, is either smooth, or vertically ridged, and becomes hollow. Edible, with a mild flavour.

Colour: pale yellow, pale brown, becoming reddish-brown; flesh and spores white.

Height: up to 12 inches; up to 2 inches thick at widest. The largest British *Clavaria*. In the U.S.A. grows to 6 inches.

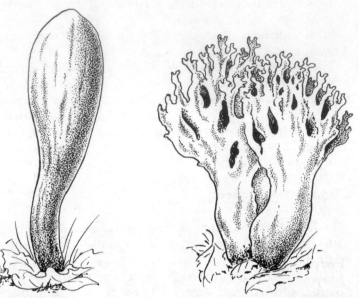

Club Clavaria *(Clavaria pistillaris)*

Purple-Tipped Coral Fungus *(Clavaria botrytis)*

Rose-Pink Coral Fungus *(Clavaria subbotrytis):*
North America.

In coniferous forest; on rich humus. Common. Late summer, autumn.

The erect, branched sporophore has rubbery or gelatinous flesh and branches rising from a thick stem base. Edible.
Colour: rosy-pink, fading to salmon-pink; flesh white; spores pinkish.
Height: up to 6 inches.

Not to be confused with the inedible Pink Coral Fungus (North America) (*Clavaria formosa*) which has fragile fibrous flesh with a slightly acrid flavour. Its branches are flesh coloured or pinkish with yellow tips, the spores yellowish. Or with the Coral Mushroom (North America) (*Clavaria gelatinosa*), a pinkish-cinnamon fungus with semi-transparent flesh and which is watery and gelatinous at its base and lower branches. Its spores are ochraceous.

222

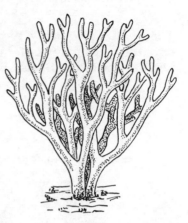

Straight Coral Fungus *(Clavaria stricta)*

Purple-Tipped Coral Fungus (North America) *(Clavaria botrytis):*
British Isles, North America.

In coniferous forest; on the ground, among moss. In groups. Common. Late summer, autumn.

The fleshy, erect sporophore has many slender branches irregularly divided, like coral. The branch tips are sharp-pointed, the stem thick. Edible, with a mild flavour. Colour: creamy-white, branch tips pinkish-red, purplish, becoming brown; flesh white or pale yellowish near tips; spores yellow.
Height: up to 6 inches.

Straight Coral Fungus (North America) *(Clavaria stricta):*
British Isles, North America.

Rotten wood, stumps and similar, the only British *Clavaria* to choose this habitat. In dense tufts. Common. Summer, autumn.

The sporophore is erect, with many branches, its base also having branched white mycelial cords. Not edible; tough, with a spicy aroma and acrid flavour.
Colour: pinkish-buff; branch tips pale yellow to buff; may have wine or violet tint.
Height: up to 4 inches.

223

SPARASSIS

This genus is quickly recognized because the sporophore resembles a cauliflower heart or large sponge. There are only two species in the British Isles.

Cauliflower Fungus (*Sparassis crispa*)

Cauliflower Fungus (*Sparassis crispa*):
British Isles.

In coniferous woodlands, or around the base of conifer trees or stumps. Fairly common. Autumn.

The sporophore has many ramifying flattened, branches lobed, curved, twisted, wavy, or curled and crisped. The short, stem-like base is attached by cord-like strands to the host tree's roots, this fungus probably being parasitic. The flesh is wax-like and fragile. Edible when young. Has a pleasant aroma.

Colour: pale cream or buff, tips becoming yellowish; base whitish becoming blackish; spores buff.

Width: up to 12 inches.

The other species, *SPARASSIS LAMINOSA* is similar, differing in the width of the branch folds and in that the branches are less densely crowded and more flattened.

THELEPHORACEAE

In the genus *Thelephoraceae* or *Skin Fungus*, the smooth, spore-bearing hymenium either covers most of the flat skin-like sporophore, or is on the lower surface of a bracket. The family contains the genera: *Thelephora*, *Stereum*, *Peniophora* and *Hymenochaete*, but as a large number of the species is extremely difficult to identify and requires microscopic examination, only the first two genera are described.

THELEPHORA

Thelephora terrestris:
British Isles.

In coniferous woodlands, on heaths; encrusting upon twigs and leaves on the ground. Common. Late summer, autumn, early winter.

Thelephora terrestris

The irregular sporophore is fan-shaped, skin-like, thin, scaly and shaggy, with a fringed margin and the spore-surface wrinkled; the spores are spiny or angular.
Colour: chocolate-brown, with a violet tint; margin paler; spore underside dark grey; spores brown.
Width: up to 2 inches.

STEREUM

The *Stereum* genus has species that are predominantly either funnel- or bracket-shaped, stalked or sessile, and could be mistaken for smaller versions of species in other families; a few, however, resemble pieces of skin.

Specimens in this genus are built in three layers – the outer shaggy skin; an inner layer of hyphae parallel to the surface; and the lower spore-bearing smooth hymenium. The brackets are attached to the habitat by a basal sheet, but in cramped conditions on the underside of timber this basal sheet alone may be present without a bracket development.

Hairy Stereum (North America) *(Stereum hirsutum):*
British Isles, North America.

Logs, posts, poles and various timbers. In tiers. Common. Throughout year.

The sporophore is usually bracket-shaped, though is sometimes funnel-shaped when on stumps; it is wavy, irregular and leathery with a hairy, zoned upper surface. Causes a fibrous white rot.

Colour: upper surface dull yellowish-grey; hymenium under-surface bright yellow-brown becoming buff, grey.

Width: up to 4 inches.

Hairy Stereum *(Stereum hirsutum)*

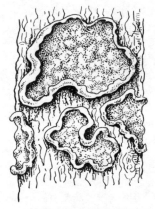

Stereum rugosum

Stereum purpureum:
British Isles.

On dead wood, branches, and living trees, especially plum, blackthorn and other *Rosaceae*; also on beech and poplar. In crusts or tiers. Very common. Throughout year.

The sporophore is either a small, projecting, semi-circular bracket on a vertical surface, or a skin-like growth on a flat surface; its upper layer being woolly. Causes silver leaf disease.

Colour: upper surface greyish or brownish; hymenium under-surface bright purple-lilac becoming buff or grey.

Width: up to 2 inches.

Stereum rugosum:
British Isles.

On stumps, logs, fallen branches, trunks; also on living trees, particularly hardwoods. Common. Throughout year.

The sporophore is flat, crusty, woody and brittle; rarely bracket-shaped. Its spore-producing surface faces upwards and its margin is upcurved.

Colour: brown; spore-producing surface yellowish-buff, then grey, but when cut or bruised stains blood-red.

Several inches in length and width.

Stereum sanguinolentum:
British Isles.

Only on conifer logs, stumps, branches, twigs. Very common. Throughout year.

The flat sporophore is skin-like when young, though when its margin later curls up it forms a bracket-shape with radiating fibrils. Resembles *Stereum rugosum* but is thinner and less woody.

Colour: greyish, fawn or buff; also bleeds red on being cut or bruised.

Several inches in length and width.

MERULIACEAE

This genus is not particularly interesting but is included because the collector will no doubt meet some of its species. It is divided into three genera – *Merulius, Coniophora* and *Phlebia.*

MERULIUS

Dry Rot Fungus *(Merulius lacrymans):*
British Isles, North America.

In buildings, mines, damp underground or unventilated constructions; on posts, under floor boards, behind panelling and similar woodwork. It is also found on brickwork and other surfaces a considerable distance from the original affected timber, since it grows strands with wide hyphae in order to take water to its dryer sub-colonies. Very common. Throughout year, but mostly summer, autumn.

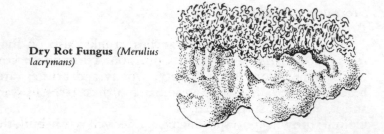

Dry Rot Fungus *(Merulius lacrymans)*

The sporophore is mainly flat, but on a vertical surface it may be bracket-shaped. The hymenium has shallow pores; the margin is sterile; and the mycelium grows in sheets or strands, exuding drops of moisture. It produces millions of spores which form a dust on the habitat.
Colour: hymenium rust-red or orange-brown; margin whitish or lilac tinted; mycelium silver-grey; spores rust-red or yellowish.
Width of colony can exceed 36 inches.

CONIOPHORA

Cellar Fungus *(Coniophora cerebella [puteana]):*
British Isles.

On the underside of logs, branches, or other debris wood lying upon the earth; also in buildings on damp, decaying timber. Very common.

228

The thin, flat, skin-like sporophore is irregularly shaped, its surface lumpy or pimply. It causes a dark brown, almost a black, crumbling rot, the affected wood perhaps having branched, root-like, dark brown mycelium strands on its surface.

Colour: hymenium surface yellowish, then olive-green or olive-brown; margin creamy-white; spores yellow-brown or olive-brown.

Width: up to 24 inches.

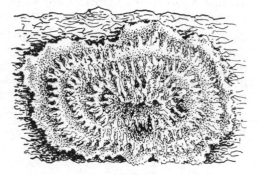

Phlebia merismoides

Phlebia merismoides:

British Isles.

Damp decaying wood, old stumps, branches, and similar. Very common. Autumn, winter.

The sporophore is a gelatinous mass which may cover an extensive area. Its hymenium is on radiating ridged veins and the flat margin is striate.

Colour: hymenium flesh pink or purplish-white; margin orange.

HYMENOMYCETES – Heterobasidiae

The *Heterobasidiae* have a basidium which is either septate or forked and they are softly gelatinous, hence their name 'Jelly Fungi'. When wet they are usually bright and conspicuous, but as they dry they become inconspicuous, shrunken and rigid, soon to recover size and colour when moistened again. There are four families – *Auriculariaceae*, *Tremellaceae*, *Caloceraceae* and *Dacrymycetaceae*.

229

AURICULARIACEAE

The *Auriculariaceae* has the hymenium on the under-surface, the basidia being transversely septate.

Jew's Ear, Ear Fungus *(Auricularia auricula judae):*
British Isles, North America.

On living or dead branches of trees, chiefly elder in British Isles and Europe, various trees in North America. In tiered groups. Common. Throughout year, especially autumn.

The irregular, somewhat limp sporophore may be shaped like an ear, a saucer, or a cup. The margins are inrolled with shallow folded surfaces, the outer velvety, the spore-producing inner surface smooth and shiny, with veins. The flesh is translucent with a texture like soft rubber. Edible. Colour: outer-surface liver-brown, red-brown, maroon, dark flesh, sometimes with olive-grey tints; inner-surface with hymenium yellowish-brown; spores white.
Width: up to 3 inches.

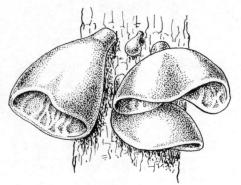

Jew's Ear, Ear Fungus
(Auricularia auricula judae)

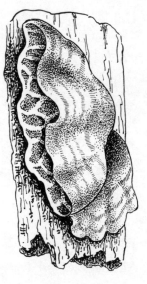

Tripe Fungus *(Auricularia mesenterica)*

230

Tripe Fungus *(Auricularia mesenterica):*
British Isles.

Old hardwood trunks, stumps, logs, large branches. In clusters. Common. Throughout year.

The sporophore is bracket-shaped with a wavy margin. The upper surface is velvety, the spore-producing under-surface gelatinous, veined and wrinkled, folded to form an irregular network.

Colour: outer surface brownish-grey with darker zoned areas; hymenium brownish-purple.

Width: up to 3 inches.

TREMELLACEAE

The *Tremellaceae* has the basidia longitudinally septate.

Witches' Butter *(Exidia glandulosa):*
British Isles.

Logs, stumps, dead branches of hardwood trees, especially oak. In groups. Common. Throughout year, especially winter.

The sporophore is rounded and gelatinous; the hymenium is covered with small raised wart-like growths.

Colour: outer surface dark grey becoming black; hymenium dark brown when young, black later.

Width: up to 2 inches.

Yellow Brain Fungus *(Tremella mesenterica):*
British Isles.

Dead branches, twigs and similar debris. In clusters. Common. Throughout year, more so late autumn, winter.

The sporophore is a soft, gelatinous mass, contorted with wavy, brain-like folds, hence its name.

Colour: bright golden- or orange-yellow.

Width: up to 3 inches.

CALOCERACEAE

Although they are tough, elastic and jelly-like, and with

forked basidia, members of this wood-hosting genus may be mistaken for *Clavaria.*

Yellow Antler Fungus *(Calocera viscosa):*
British Isles.

Coniferous woodlands; on pine stumps and debris. Singly or in groups. Very common. Autumn, winter.

The sporophore has several long, erect and flattened branches like a stag's antlers, slimy when wet, tough and horny when dry.
Colour: egg- or orange-yellow; spores yellow.
Height: up to 3 inches.
The related *Calocera cornea* is similar, but smaller and paler and grows in tufts; *Calocera stricta* is also yellow but is never branched and grows singly.

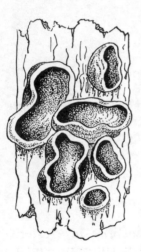

Witches' Butter *(Exidia glandulosa)*

Yellow Brain Fungus *(Tremella mesenterica)*

232

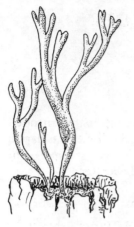

Yellow Antler Fungus *(Calocera viscosa)*

Dacrymyces Deliquescens

DACRYMYCETACEAE

A genus which has the basidium divided or deeply forked.

Dacrymyces Deliquescens:
British Isles.

On wet, rotten wood, old softwood fences, etc. In groups. Common. Throughout year.

The small, rounded, cushion–like sporophore has gelatinous lumps and may grow in colonies along the cracks in its habitat; in dry weather it shrinks almost to vanishing point. Colour: yellow or orange.

Width: up to $\frac{1}{8}$ inch.

A related species is the not–so–soft, deep orange *Dacrymyces stillatus*.

5 Ascomycetes

The *Ascomycetes* or Sac Fungi produce their spores in minute, closed tubes or sacs, known as asci, as described in Chapter Two. The *Ascomycetes* are divided into three groups – the *Discomycetes*, the *Pyrenomycetes* and the *Tuberaceae*.

DISCOMYCETES

The *Discomycetes* have their asci forming a hymenium on the fruiting body surface exposed to the air. The group is subdivided into the *Pezizaceae*, the *Geoglossaceae* and *Helvellaceae*.

PEZIZACEAE

The *Pezizaceae* or Cup Fungi have, as their name indicates, a cup-shaped fruit body when young. The ripe spores, being unable to fall because of this shape, are discharged violently upwards, in some species the merest touch or zephyr being enough to trigger the action.

Brown Elf Cup *(Peziza [Aleuria] vesiculosa)*

Brown Elf Cup *(Peziza [Aleuria] vesiculosa):*
British Isles.
   Old manure heaps and other rich soil. In groups. Common. Spring, summer, late autumn.

The sporophore's bladder-shaped cup becomes irregular, fleshy, fragile, inside smooth, outside scaly; margin incurved, waved, notched.

Colour: interior pale brown, exterior whitish or pale yellowish.

Width: up to 2 inches.

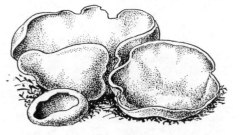

Orange Peel Fungus *(Peziza [Aleuria] aurantia)*

Orange Peel Fungus (British Isles), Orange Elf Cup (British Isles), Orange Fairy Cup (North America), Orange Cup Fungus (North America) *(Peziza [Aleuria] aurantia)*:

British Isles, North America.

In damp woodlands, on hedge-banks, earth paths, sometimes along stream-banks; on bare soil. In close groups. Common. Late summer, autumn, early winter.

The sporophore's cupola shape is at first almost closed, later expanding until it becomes completely flattened, with an irregular, wavy and lobed – but smooth – upper surface; the under-surface is seen under a magnifying glass to be downy. The margin is sometimes split; the minute stem attached centrally to its habitat and the flesh thin and fragile. Edible.

Colour: bright orange, resembling orange peel; underside paler or whitish.

Width: up to 5 inches.

Other similar species are:

Peziza repanda, found growing in the autumn on wood, frequently even on sawdust, and recognized by its pale chestnut-brown interior and pale fawn exterior;

Peziza varia, a woodland species of the summer and autumn

235

months with a pale, greyish-brown interior that darkens on maturity;

Peziza badia, another woodland species of the summer and autumn which has a dark brown interior and paler brown exterior; and

Peziza anthrocophila, found on burnt soil and woodland fire sites from late spring until autumn and identified by its dark brown interior.

Scarlet Elf Cup, Red Cup Fungus *(Sarcoscypha [Plectania] coccinea)*

Scarlet Elf Cup (British Isles), Red Cup Fungus (North America) *(Sarcoscypha [Plectania] coccinea):*
British Isles, North America.

On dead, decaying wood, brushwood and other debris. In groups. Common. Winter, early spring.

The sporophore is a stalked cup, rather like a goblet, and has a downy exterior.

Colour: interior bright scarlet-red or crimson-red, exterior whitish or pinkish-white.

Height: up to 1 inch; cup up to 1 inch in diameter.

Scented Elf Cup *(Peziza venosa):*
British Isles.

On the ground. In groups. Fairly common. Spring.

The cup-shaped sporophore has ribs radiating from its base. Its powerful nitrous aroma is a vital clue to its identification.

Colour: interior umber-brown, exterior whitish-brown.

Width: up to 3 inches.

OTIDEA

This genus is also included in the *Pezizaceae* although its sporophores are not distinctly cup shaped, looking instead like a hare's ear.

Hare's Ear *(Otidea leporina):*
British Isles.

Woodlands; among dead leaves, especially spruce needles. In clusters. Fairly common. Autumn.

The sporophore is Hare's ear-shaped when young, then long and upright with notched margins and a scurfy exterior. Colour: interior cinnamon- or rust-brown; exterior yellowish.

Height: up to 2 inches.

Hare's Ear *(Otidea leporina)*

Lemon Peel Fungus *(Otidea onotica)*

Lemon Peel Fungus *(Otidea onotica):*
British Isles.

Broadleafed woodlands, especially oak; among dead leaves. In groups. Fairly common. Early autumn.

The sporophore is approximately rabbits' ear- or scoop-shaped with notched margins and mealy exterior. Colour: yellow interior with a pinkish tint, exterior with a pale brown tint.

Height: up to 3 inches.

GEOGLOSSACEAE

This family, otherwise known as Earth Tongue, has a club-shaped, narrow-stemmed sporophore, sometimes flattened.

Smooth Earth Tongue *(Geoglossum difforme [cookeianum])*

Smooth Earth Tongue (North America) *(Geoglossum difforme [cookeianum]):*
British Isles, North America.
 In damp pastures, among short, mossy grass. In tufts. Fairly common. Summer.
 The sporophores of this fungus are caespitose – they grow together in clusters – somewhat bent, and viscid; they may also be poisonous.
Colour: dark olive-green or blackish.
Height: up to 3 inches.

HELVELLACEAE

The typical sporophore of this family is a wrinkled cone or ball on a stout, thick stem. There are four genera: *Morchella, Gyromitra, Verpa,* and *Helvella.*

MORCHELLA

This genus is easily recognized by its sponge – or

238

honeycomb-like pitted cap and its fragile and hollow stem.
The hymenium is found as a lining in the pits.

Common Morel *(Morchella esculenta)*

Common Morel *(Morchella esculenta):*
British Isles, North America.

Among hedgerow bases, in clearings in woodlands and on
banks; on rich soil, or on disturbed ground where wood or
paper has been burned. Singly. Fairly common. Spring.

The hollow cap is rounded or egg-shaped, with irregular
cavities separated by prominent, sinuous ribs joined laterally.
The mealy stem is quite short, stout, very brittle and hollow,
and may be grooved near its base. Edible, it was formerly
widely used for flavouring when dried.

Colour: variable; pale ochreous-yellow, pale brown,
blackish-grey; hymenium surface darker brown; stem
yellowish-white.

Height: up to 6 inches; cap up to 3 inches in diameter.

GYROMITRA

This genus differs from *Morchella* in that its hymenium is
convoluted and its cap more folded and irregularly shaped. In

North America *Gyromitra* is known as the False Morel, a term which in the British Isles applies to the *Helvella*.

Brain Gyromitra (North America), False Morel (North America) *(Gyromitra esculenta):*
British Isles, North America.
 Damp woodland, particularly coniferous; on sandy soil. Singly or in small groups. Not common in England, more so in Scotland. Fairly common North America. Spring, summer.

Brain Gyromitra, False Morel
(Gyomitra esculenta)

 The irregular-shaped cap is rounded at its summit, and is mop-like and contorted with brain-like convolutions, hence its name; the thick, brittle, smooth stem is hollow, though may be solid at its base. It is sometimes grooved. Poisonous if eaten raw; questionably edible after careful boiling.
Colour: cap reddish-brown, chocolate-brown, dark brown; stem whitish-grey; spores yellowish.
Height: up to 4 inches; cap up to 5 inches in diameter.

VERPA

This genus has a bell-shaped cap, the base of which is free from the long, cylindrical stem growing from the centre.

240

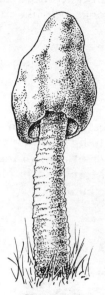

Early Morel *(Verpa bohemica)*

Verpa conica

Early Morel (North America) *(Verpa bohemica):*
North America.

On soil near trees. Singly or scattered in small groups.
Common. Spring, summer.

The thimble–shaped cap has thick, rounded, longitudinal
folds and a skirt-like base free from the cylindrical, brittle,
hollow stem. Questionably edible.
Colour: cap tan or brown, finally blackish; stem white or
cream.
Height: up to 7 inches; cap up to 2 inches in diameter.

Verpa conica:
British Isles.

On grassland and among heather; on sandy soil. Singly or
scattered. Fairly common. Spring.

The cap is conical, ridged and lobed, its hymenium on

241

ridges and in cavities; the cap's margin is close to but free from the smooth, short, stout stem which, with its granular, transverse, belt–like markings, is brittle.
Colour: cap brown; stem yellowish, belt–like markings reddish–yellow.
Height: up to 3 inches.

HELVELLA

Members of this genus have a variety of cap shapes, usually resembling a saddle, or folded irregularly: the stems have a number of ribs. In the British Isles *Helvella* is known as the False Morel, but in North America goes under the name of Saddle Fungus.

Elf's Saddle *(Helvella lacunosa)*

Helvella crispa

Elf's Saddle *(Helvella lacunosa):*
British Isles, North America.
In broadleafed woodlands, usually on burnt ground. Singly or scattered in groups. Common. Autumn.

The cap is saddle-shaped, with two lobes and irregular folds. Thin and fragile, its margins curve under to the hollow, deeply grooved stem. Edible only when cooked young, when it has a flavour like Morel.

Colour: cap medium-grey to dark greyish-black; stem whitish or ash-grey; flesh dark grey, lavender tinted.

Height: up to 6 inches; cap up to 2 inches wide.

Helvella crispa:

British Isles.

Damp woodlands, among grass, along tracks and paths. Singly. Common. Spring, late summer, early autumn.

The saddle-shaped, lobed cap is folded irregularly and is wavy; the hollow stem is stout and lacunose with deep, elongated grooves and coarse ribs, and may taper upwards from its wide base. Not edible.

Colour: cap pale whitish-grey or cream; stem white; flesh cream.

Height: up to 4 inches.

PYRENOMYCETES

The *Pyrenomycetes* is a very large group in the *Ascomycetes*, the majority of the species being small to minute, so it is only possible to identify them by using a microscope. Only the larger species are included as being more likely to be found by the amateur collector: these are in two groups; *Sphaeriales* and *Hypocreales*.

SPHAERIALES

The *Sphaeriales* have sporophores which are hard and carbonaceous and are divided into four genera: *Daldinia*, *Xylosphaera* (*Xylaria*), *Ustulina* and *Hypoxylon*. Their anatomy is described in Chapter One.

DALDINIA

The sporophores of this genus are cushion-like or rounded, with concentric rings or zone markings that are exposed if the specimen is cut in half.

King Alfred's Cakes (British Isles), Cramp Balls (British Isles) *(Daldinia concentrica):*
British Isles, North America.

Dead trunks and branches of ash and occasionally other hardwoods. Common. Singly or several together. Throughout year, especially early autumn, winter.

King Alfred's Cakes
(Daldinia concentrica)

The rounded, hard, smooth sporophore is shiny as it matures, storing water so it can discharge its spores in a period of drought; the flesh is also hard. This fungus is responsible for the whitish dark spotted rot in ash timber, which is then known as calico wood. One of its names derives from the rural belief that specimens carried in the clothing prevented cramp, ague and other rheumatic conditions.
Colour: dark reddish or chocolate-brown when young, becoming black; after spore discharge in summer it appears to be covered by soot; flesh purplish-brown, with alternating light and dark zones; spores black.
Diameter: up to $2\frac{1}{2}$ inches.

XYLOSPHAERA (XYLARIA)

Specimens of this genus have erect, single or multiple-branching, sporophores which are either cylindrical or club-shaped. The perithecia is in the upper portion's surface layer where the spore-containing asci form, though in some species there is an early stage, producing a coating of powdery white asexually-formed spores known as conidia.

244

Candle Snuff Fungus *(Xylosphaera [Xylaria] hypoxylon):*
British Isles.

Dead, rotting wood, hardwood stumps, fallen branches, logs. Sometimes in large groups. Very common. Throughout year.

The erect, antler–shaped sporophore may be branched or unbranched, but is forked at the tips, and is tough. The flattened stems are straight.

Colour: sporophore, tips at first pale grey covered with a powder of white spores – the conidia – the tips later blacken as the perithecia develop. A hand lens examination of the surface reveals the covering of raised openings of the tiny, flask–shaped cavities in which the black spores develop. Stem black; flesh white.

Height: up to 2 inches.

Candle Snuff Fungus
(Xylosphaera [Xylaria]
hypoxylon)

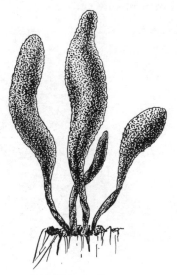

Dead Man's Fingers
(Xylosphaera [Xylaria]
polymorpha)

Dead Man's Fingers *(Xylosphaera [Xylaria] polymorpha):*
British Isles, North America.

Old tree stumps, especially beech, usually at soil level; and other dead wood, sometimes buried. In groups. Common. Throughout year.

The club-shaped or finger-like sporophore is hard, its upper portion irregular and swollen. The short, wavy stem has a smooth upper section when young, with a covering of pale brown spores – the conidia – but it becomes rough as the protruding, flask-shaped spore-producing cavities (the perithecia) develop: these can be seen clearly in a cross-section. The fungus causes root-rot in apple and other trees.
Colour: sporophore dull black; flesh white; spores black.
Height: up to 3 inches; up to 1 inch thick in centre.

USTULINA

Ustulina deusta:
British Isles. The only British representative of the genus.
  Old hardwood stumps and dead roots. Fairly common. Throughout year.

Ustulina deusta

The sporophore is a thick, spreading, irregular crust; when young it appears powdery due to the conidia on its surface, but the surface becomes pimply as the tips of the perithecia develop; as it ages the crust becomes brittle and may flake away.

246

Colour: greyish-brown when young, then black; flesh white; spores black.
Size variable.

HYPOXYLON

Hypoxylon fragiliforme:
British Isles.

Dead trunks, branches, felled timber, of hardwoods, especially beech. Very numerous on habitat. Common. Autumn, winter.

Hypoxylon fragiliforme

The sporophore is rounded, almost spherical, and hard, similar to *Daldinia* but much smaller and not having the concentric zones. The flesh is brittle.
Colour: salmon-pink when young, then brick-red, finally dark-brown or blackish; flesh dark brown or blackish.
Width: up to $\frac{1}{2}$ inch.

HYPOCREALES

The softer sporophores of *Hypocreales* are found in a variety of colours, except black.

Coral Spot Fungus *(Nectria cinnabarina):*
British Isles, North America.

On damp, fallen hardwood twigs, old pea sticks, etc. In colonies. Common. Throughout year.

The granular sporophore is spherical or cushion-like, and dusted with immature spores, becoming darker and warty as the perithecia develop.

Colour: pink when young, powdery, becoming dark cinnabar red.
Width: up to $\frac{1}{8}$ inch.

Coral Spot Fungus *(Nectria cinnabarina)*

Vegetable Caterpillar
(Cordyceps militaris)

Vegetable Caterpillar (North America) *(Cordyceps militaris):*

British Isles, North America.

A parasite of insect larvae and pupae, found singly or in small groups in grass. Fairly common. Autumn.

The clubbed, plume-like, waxy sporophore narrows at each end, the fertile upper portion being punctured with the perithecia openings: the stem may be either wavy or curved. The mummified case, usually of a moth or butterfly larva, and filled with a solid mycelium mass, will be found at the base of each fungus, since when a spore adheres to the moist skin of a caterpillar, its fate is sealed.
Colour: bright crimson.
Height: up to 2 inches.

TUBERACEAE

This, a special family in the *Ascomycetes*, consists of subterranean fungi divided into two genera: the *Terfezia* and the *Tuber*. While there are only doubtful records of *Terfezia* occurring in the British Isles, several species of *Tuber* – better known as Truffles – are found here, and in the past some were

248

eagerly sought since they were more highly esteemed than Mushrooms. They usually lie at least three or four inches deep in the soil, thus creating problems in locating them, though one of the indications to their presence is that they sometimes push towards the surface when nearing maturity and may be detected by small cracks in the soil which could radiate from a tiny molehill–like mound.

It is well known that on the Continent, pigs and dogs are trained to sniff out Truffles, but it is less known that certain water diviners claim to be able to locate them.

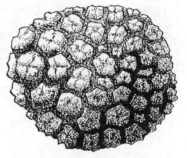

Summer Truffle *(Tuber aestivum)*

These delectable fungi also form part of the regular diet of the woodland fauna – squirrels, rats, badgers, mice and deer – and their diggings, particularly when on chalky soils, may be another vital clue to the human Truffle collector. A less appetizing clue to the Truffle's presence is the sight of a swarm of flies – *Helomyza tubivora* or *H. lineata* – hovering about a foot above the ground preparatory to laying their eggs in the fungus.

The complete history of Truffles as food for man, and his methods of locating them, are excellently described by John Ramsbottom in his *Mushrooms and Toadstools*.

TUBER

The genus *Tuber* has rounded or tuber-shaped sporophores, the peridium smooth or warty and the inside a network of veins, the darker veins being the hymenium, and up to four globose or reticulate ovoid spores are formed within the oval or rounded asci. The sporophore's flesh has a marbled appearance.

Summer Truffle *(Tuber aestivum):*
British Isles, North America.

In woodlands, on calcareous soil, mainly under beeches. Singly. Fairly common. Summer, autumn.

The irregular, globular sporophore is covered with large, hard and prominent pyramid-shaped warts each with four to six distinct faces. Set in rough horizontal rows, these warts thus create an irregularly grooved surface to the truffle, the interior of which has a network of veins. Edible, with a slight but pleasant aroma and a nutty flavour.
Colour: dark brown, purplish-black or bluish-black when fresh, becoming brownish-black as it ages; flesh yellowish-white at first, then greyish-buff or brownish with a violet tint; interior vein network whitish.
Width: up to 4 inches.

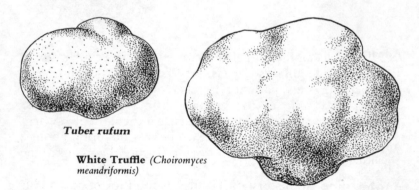

Tuber rufum

White Truffle *(Choiromyces meandriformis)*

Tuber rufum:
British Isles.

In broadleafed and coniferous woodlands. Singly. Fairly common. Summer.

Similar to *Tuber aestivum* but smaller, its sporophore is minutely warted. Edible, with a nutty flavour.
Colour: reddish-brown; flesh greyish-lilac.
Width: up to 1 inch.

White Truffle *(Choiromyces meandriformis):*
British Isles.

In oaklands, usually half-buried. Singly. Fairly common.
Summer.

The sporophore is globular with a ridged base and nodules;
the flesh is hard and there are numerous hymenial veins, eight
round, spiny spores are contained in the ascus. Edible.
Colour: creamy-white, then pale reddish-brown; the surface
may have white lines; flesh whitish becoming yellowish; veins
ochraceous.
Width: up to 5 inches.

Quick Reference Glossary of Text Terms

Adnate A type of gill which is broadly attached to the stem at its inner end, as in *Stropharia* (see Illustrated Glossary).

Adnexed A gill type which just reaches the stem, to which it is finely attached, as in *Amanita rubescens.* A close examination is sometimes required to distinguish from Free Gills (see Illustrated Glossary).

Adpressed Flattened fibrils or scales that are pressed together without being joined.

Amyloid A spore mass that becomes blue-black when wet with solutions of iodine; starchy.

Anastomosis, anastomosing Gills which repeatedly fork and run together to form a network.

Annulate A stem having a ring or annulus.

Annulus The membranous ring occurring on the mature stems of some species.

Apothecium The open cup or saucer-like fertile part of a *Discomycete.*

Arcuate Bow-shaped gills.

Ascospore A spore formed in the Ascus.

Ascus (pl. **asci**) The microscopic, swollen, closed sac-like end structure of hyphae in which the spores of *Ascomycetes* are formed.

Basidiospore A spore formed on a Basidium.

Basidium (pl. **basidia**) The microscopic cell which bears sexual spores on sterigmata in the *Basidiomycetes*.

Caespitose Growing together in clusters or tufts.

Campanulate Bell-shaped.

Capillitium Sterile threads that are mixed with spores in the gleba of the *Gasteromycetes*.

Cartilaginous The flexible, tough, rubbery, elastic or gristly quality of stems which bend without cracking or snapping; resembling cartilage in texture.

Chlamydospore A rounded mycelium cell or spore that is asexual and thick-walled.

Clavate Shaped like a club.

Columella A column, usually small, of sterile tissue that extends upwards into the gleba in some species of the *Gasteromycetes*.

Context The fleshy inner portion of cap or pileus.

Coprophilous A species that grows on manure.

Coriaceous Leathery, tough.

Cortina The cobweb-like partial veil of some species, especially the *Cortinarius*, which sometimes leaves a zone on the stem. It is most evident in young examples.

Crisped Finely curled or crinkled.

Cystidium The sterile end of a hypha in the hymenium, sometimes having a thick wall.

Decurrent Gills which continue down the stem, as in *Lactarius* (see Illustrated Glossary).

Deliquescent Liquefying; dissolving; in the process of melting; becoming liquid in air.

Dichotomous Branching into pairs.

Dimidiate Divided into two unequal parts.

Emarginate Gills with a deep curve or notch at their end close to where attached to the stem (see *Sinuate*).

Endoperidium The inner layer of the peridium in the *Gasteromycetes*; opposite of exoperidium.

Enzyme A chemical ferment secreted by an organism; a ferment contrasted with yeast and other organic ferments.

Evanescent Transitory; fleeting; disappearing; not persistent or permanent and so occurring for a short period only.

Excentric, eccentric One-sided; off centre.

Exoperidium The outer layer of the peridium in the *Gasteromycetes.*

Ferruginous Rust coloured.

Fibrillose Covered with or composed of small parallel, silky fibres, particularly on the surface of the cap of certain species.

Fibrous A stem with a stringy, thread-like texture resembling fibres.

Fimbriated With a border or fringe; applying in particular to the cap margin when the partial veil stays attached to it instead of to the stem.

Fleshy The nature of a thick cap or stem which quickly breaks when bent.

Floccose Tufty; fluffy; woolly.

Free Gills which are not attached to the stem.

Funiculus The slender thread-like stalk attaching the peridioles to the peridium of Bird's Nest Fungi.

Gills The radiating, vertical, plate-like structures carrying the hymenium, sited on the underside of the caps of the *Agaricaceae.*

Gleba The soft inner tissue of the peridium of the *Gasteromycetes,* containing spores and sterile tissue.

Granulous, granulose Consisting of or resembling small particles or granules.

Habit The usual appearance and development of a species in the wild.

Habitat The usual location of a species in the wild.

Hirsute Shaggy; hairy; bearded.

Hispid Covered with long, stiff, bristly hairs.

Hyaline Glassy; transparent; translucent; colourless.

Hygrophanous Caps which appear to be soaked with water when wet, but which turn pale and opaque as the pileus surface dries.

Hymenium The spore-bearing layer of tissue or organs upon the surface of gills or tubes.

Hypha (pl. **hyphae**) The tiny filaments from which the mycelium and fruiting body are built.

Imbricated Overlapped, like tiles on a roof.

Indusium Outer case of a spore cluster.

Involuted The inward-rolled edges of caps.

Lacunose With small pits or cavities.

Lamella (pl. **lamellae**) The thin plates or gills.

Lateral A stem growing on the side of the cap.

Latex Milky juice found in some fungi.

Mycelium The mass of vegetative hyphae comprising the main body of a fungus and situated in soil or other habitat; the 'spawn' of fungi.

Mycology The scientific study of fungi.

Mycorrhiza The partnership between fungi and the roots of other plants, such as wild orchids.

Ochraceous Yellow-brown.

Paraphysis (pl. **paraphyses**) The sterile threads between basidia or asci in a hymenium.

Parasites Organisms which live upon or within another organism and obtain nourishment from their host.

Partial A type of veil that extends from the cap edge to the stem.

Pellicle The thin, skin-like outer layer of the cap.

Peridioles The small, round bodies containing the spores in the *Nidulariaceae*.

Peridium The outer covering or wall of the *gleba*, the spore-bearing tissue, in the *Gasteromycetes*.

Perithecium (pl. **perithecia**) The minute flask-like or rounded structures containing the *asci* in the *Pyrenomycetes*.

Pileus The spore-bearing cap of *Agaric* fungi.

Plicate Having folds or ridges.

Pore The opening of the tiny spore-bearing tubule in a Polypore, and fungi such as *Boletus*.

Pruinose Having a white bloom like hoar-frost.

Radicating Having a tapering root-like extension at the base of the *stipe*.

Receptacle An axis that is bearing one or more organs; a hymenium-bearing structure.

Remote Gills which have a gap between them and the stem, as in *Lepiota*.

Reticulate Patterned like a net.

Rhizomorph A root-like structure composed of hyphae, sometimes visible at the stipe's base.

Saprophytes Fungi that live on decaying organic matter, such as dead insect or animal remains.

Sclerotium (pl. **sclerotia**) A dormant, rounded, compacted mass of hyphae.

Septate Having septa – dividing partitions.

Septum (pl. **septa**) A dividing partition or cell wall.

Sessile A type of cap attached directly to its habitat without a stem.

Seta (pl. **setae**) A stiff, thick, pointed hair or cystidium.

Simple Undivided; unbranched.

Sinuate A type of gill which curves upwards near the point of attachment to the stem, as in *Entoloma, Tricholoma* (see *Emarginate*).

Spore The minute reproductive body of a fungus, akin to a seed in the flowering plants.

Sporophore The fruit or spore-producing body of fungi.

Sterigma (pl. **sterigmata**) The small, thin points or stalks on the basidia which bears the spores.

Stipe The stem or stalk-like part of a fruiting fungus.

Stipitate Having a stipe.

Striate Having fine lines, longitudinal streaks, or minute grooves; usually close to the rim of the pileus, or on the stipe.

Stroma A compact, sometimes hard, cushiony body of hyphae in which the perithecia containing the asci or spore-bearing sacs are embedded in *Pyrenomycetes.*

Stuffed A type of stem having a distinct soft central area, which may disappear as the fungus ages, perhaps allowing the stem to become hollow.

Tomentose Covered with long or densely matted soft hairs.

Trama A fleshy layer just below the hymenium.

Troops Fungi which grow in a colony, but which do not develop from the same point of the mycelium (see *Tufted*).

Tufted A type of fungus which grows in a colony, and which does develop from the same point of the mycelium. Opposite of troops.

Umbilicate A type of cap with a small depression at its centre.

Umbo The convex centre of the cap.

Umbonate Having an umbo.

Undulate, undulating Wavy; having a wavy margin.

Universal A type of veil that completely envelops the young sporophore.

Veil The outer envelope or membrane that covers some of the *Agaricaceae* at the beginning of their development.

Viscid Sticky. Caps or stipes that are covered with slime when wet become sticky as it dries.

Volva A sheath-like cover or universal veil which envelops some species in their early development. It survives as a cupulate remnant or torn fragments, at the base of the stem.

Zonate Marked with zones or bands, often in the shape of concentric rings on the surface of the pileus.

Zone A girdle.

Spore Colour Aid to Classification

White, Creamy, Yellow or Pale Coloured Spores:
Amanitaceae, Lepiotae, Tricholomataceae, Pleurotaceae, Hygrophoraceae, Russulaceae, Cantharellaceae, Polyporaceae-Polyporus, Polyporaceae-Fomes, Polporaceae-Polystictus, Clavariaceae-Clavaria, Auriculariaceae, Helvellaceae-Gyromitra.

Pink Spores:
Rhodophyllaceae, Clitopilaceae, Volvariaceae, Boletaceae-Tylopilus.

True Brown Spores:
Cortinariaceae, Bolbitiaceae, Crepidotus, Boletaceae-Paxillus, Boletaceae-Boletus, Thelephoraceae-Thelephora, Meruliaceae, Lycoperdaceae-Lycoperdon.

Brownish–Black, Purplish–Brown, Purplish–Black, Black Spores:
Gomphidiaceae, Strophariaceae, Coprinaceae, Agaricaceae, Lycoperdaceae-Lycoperdon, Bovista, Calvatia, Geastraceae-Geastrum, Scleroderma, Pyrenomycetes-Daldinia, Xylosphaera, Ustulina.

Habitats Aid to Identification

Woodland – Open, Broadleafed, Hardwood, Mixed, Copse

Caesar's Amanita
Death Cap
Destroying Angel
False Death Cap
Fly Agaric
Fool's Mushroom
Panther Cap
The Blusher
White-veiled Amanita
Grisette
Devil's Boletus
Lurid Boletus
Red-cracked Boletus
Yellow-cracked Boletus
Bitter Boletus
Common Hydnum
Ashy Coral Fungus
Club Clavaria
Orange Peel Fungus
Hare's Ear
Lemon Peel Fungus
Common Morel
Brain Gyromitra
Elf's Saddle
Helvella crispa

Summer Truffle
Tuber rufum
White Truffle
Collared Stinkhorn
Columnar Stinkhorn
Common Stinkhorn
Dog Stinkhorn
Lattice Stinkhorn
Beautiful Puffball
Common Puffball
Spiny Puffball
Giant Puffball
Crowned Earth Star
Earth Star
Geastrum fimbriatum
Common Earth Ball
Scleroderma verrucosum
Nidularia pisiformis
Nidularia confluens
Common Bird's Nest
Striate Bird's Nest
Cyathus olla

Conifer Forest or under Conifer
  Trees

Fly Agaric
Grey-Brown Amanita
Panther Cap
The Blusher
White-veiled Amanita
Grisette
Tawny Grisette
Pine Mushroom
Equestrian Tricholoma
Grey Tricholoma
Leopard Tricholoma
Red-haired Tricholoma
Soap-scented Tricholoma
Tricholoma portentosum
Tricholoma psammopus
Club-footed Clitocybe
Fragrant Clitocybe
Giant Clitocybe
Orange Clitocybe
Tawny Funnel Cap
Spotted Tough Shank
Black-stemmed Marasmius
Garlic-scented Marasmius
Garlic Marasmius
Ivory Wax Cap
Emetic Russula
Russula sardonia/drimeia
Delicious Lactarius
Reddish Lactarius
Blood-red Cortinarius
Cinnamon Cortinarius
Red-gilled Cortinarius
Violet Cortinarius
Gymnopilus penetrans
Earth-leaf Inocybe
Gomphidius rutilus
Peg-top Gomphidius
Bleeding Agaricus
Red-staining Mushroom
Wood Mushroom
Chanterelle
Clustered Chanterelle
Paxillus involutus
Cep
Yellow-brown Boletus

Club Clavaria
Rose-Pink Coral Fungus
Purple-tipped Coral Fungus
Cauliflower Fungus
Thelephora terrestris
Yellow Antler Fungus
Brain Gyromitra
Tuber rufum
Crowned Earth Star

259

On Tree Trunks, Logs, Fallen Branches, Twigs, Posts, Fences and Similar

Beech Tuft
Honey Tuft
Red-haired Tricholoma
Deceiving Clitocybe
Broadleafed Collybia
Bunched Collybia
Velvet Shank
Twig Marasmius
Wood Woolly Foot
Bleeding Mycena
Capped Mycena
Mycena inclinata
Milk Drop Mycena
Orange Bonnet
White Bonnet
Roof Nail
Angel Wings
Oyster Mushroom
Pleurotus cornucopiae
Pleurotus corticatus
Sapid Pleurotus
Leathery Panus
Astringent Panus
Scaly Lentinus
Lentinellus cochleatus
Common Split Gill
Rhodotus palmatus
Silky Volvaria
Deer Toadstool
Gymnopilus penetrans
Pholiota mutabilis
Rough Pholiota
Crepidotus variabilis
Soft Slipper Toadstool
Brick-red Hypholoma
Sulphur Tuft
Glistening Ink Cap
Graceful Brittle Cap
Birch Polypore
Dryad's Saddle
Giant Polypore
Sulphur Polypore
Beef-steak Fungus
Elm Fomes

Fomes annosus
Rusty-hoof Fomes
Fir Polystictus
Multi-zoned Polystictus
Blushing Trametes
Trametes gibbosa
Oak Daedalea
Birch Lenzites
Straight Coral Fungus
Thelephora terrestris
Hairy Stereum
Stereum purpureum
Stereum rugosum
Stereum sanguinolentum
Cellar Fungus
Phlebia merismoides
Jew's Ear
Tripe Fungus
Witches' Butter
Yellow Brain Fungus
Yellow Antler Fungus
Dacrymyces deliquescens
Scarlet Elf Cup
King Alfred's Cakes/Cramp Balls
Candle Snuff Fungus
Dead Man's Fingers
Ustulina deusta
Hypoxylon fragiforme
Coral Spot Fungus
Dog Stinkhorn
Stump Puffball
White Bird's-Nest
Common Bird's-Nest
Striate Bird's-Nest
Cyathus olla

Grassy Places – fields, meadows, pastures, hedge–banks, down-land, heaths, parkland, roadside verges, lawns, golf courses and similar

Death Cap
Panther Cap
White-veiled Amanita
Grisette
Tawny Grisette
Crested Lepiota
Morgan's Lepiota
Parasol
Smooth Lepiota
Blewit
St George's Mushroom
Clitocybe dealbata
False Champignon
Clitocybe vibecina
Common Funnel Cap
Giant Clitocybe
Orange Clitocybe
Waxy Laccaria
Fairy Ring Champignon
Mycena avenacea
Omphalia ericetorum/umbellifera
Buff Cap
Conical Hygrophorus
Golden Wax Cap
Hygrophorus nigrescens
Hygrophorus obrusseus
Hygrophorus virgineus
Parrot Wax Cap
Scarlet Wax Cap
Encrusted Russula
Delicious Lactarius
Ugly Milk Cap
Woolly Milk Cap
Leptonia serrulata
The Miller
Cortinarius pholideus
Red-gilled Cortinarius
Yellow Pholiota
Fairy Cake Hebeloma
Earth-leaf Inocybe
Common Naucoria
Yellow Cow-pat Toadstool

Agrocybe praecox
Dung Roundhead
Verdigris Agaric
Liberty Cap
Common Ink Cap
Shaggy Ink Cap
Weeping Widow
Field/Meadow Mushroom
Horse Mushroom
Yellow-staining Mushroom
Boletus bovinus
Boletus variegatus
Brown Birch Boletus
Red-cracked Boletus
Yellow-cracked Boletus
Clavaria fusiformis
Orange-Peel Fungus
Smooth Earth Tongue
Common Morel
Verpa conica
Lattice Stinkhorn
Beautiful Puffball
Common Puffball
Lycoperdon hiemale/depressum
Small Round Puffball
Bovista plumbea
Giant Puffball
Mosaic Puffball
Common Earth Ball

Gardens and Lawns (See also Grassland species)

Lepiota acutesquamosa
Ragged Parasol
Fairy Cake Hebeloma
Yellow Cow-pat Toadstool
Dung Roundhead
Common Ink Cap
Columnar Stinkhorn
Common Stinkhorn
Lattice Stinkhorn
Beautiful Puffball
Common Puffball
Small Round Puffball
Nidularia pisiformis
Nidularia confluens

Common Bird's-Nest
Striate Bird's-Nest
Cyathus olla

Compost and Manure Heaps

Ragged Parasol
Wood Blewits
Handsome Volvaria
Yellow Cow-pat Toadstool
Brown Elf Cup
Giant Puffball
Dung Roundhead
Dungheap Ink Cap
Bell-shaped Mottle Gill
Butterfly Panaeolus
Panaeolus semiovatus

On Old, Decaying Fungi

Collybia tuberosa
Collybia cirrhata
Asterophora lycoperdiodes
Asterophora parasitica
Boletus parasiticus

Some Recommended Books for Further Study

Mushrooms and Toadstools, by John Ramsbottom (Collins)
Wayside and Woodland Fungi, by W. P. K. Findlay (Warne)
Poisonous Fungi, by John Ramsbottom (Penguin Books)
Edible Fungi, by John Ramsbottom (Penguin Books)
Observer's Book of Common Fungi, by E. M. Wakefield (Warne)
The Oxford Book of Flowerless Plants, by F. H. Brightman (O.U.P.)
Edible and Poisonous Fungi, Bulletin No. 23 (Ministry of Agriculture, Fisheries and Food)
Non-Flowering Plants (containing a section on fungi), by Shuttleworth and Zim (Golden Press, New York)

Index